T0313286

From Oil to Knowledge

Transforming the United Arab Emirates into a
Knowledge-Based Economy towards UAE Vision 2021

FROM OIL TO KNOWLEDGE

Transforming the United Arab Emirates into a Knowledge-Based Economy

ALLAM AHMED AND IBRAHIM ALFAKI

Routledge
Taylor & Francis Group

LONDON AND NEW YORK

First published 2016 by Greenleaf Publishing Limited

Published 2017 by Routledge
2 Park Square, Milton Park, Abingdon, Oxon OX14 4RN
711 Third Avenue, New York, NY 10017, USA

Routledge is an imprint of the Taylor & Francis Group, an informa business

British Library Cataloguing in Publication Data:
    A catalogue record for this book is available from the British Library.

    ISBN-13: 978-1-78353-357-2 [hbk]

Contents

UAE: FROM
OIL TO KNOWLEDGE

1 CHAPTER

INTRODUCTION

INTRODUCTION

"Ninety-nine per cent of the work people do is knowledge-based"
(Wah, 1999)

Managing knowledge, improving the capability people have to learn together and creating processes to increase human and social capital seem to have become the most crucial success factors in competition between nations. Many nations have gained significant benefits from investing in Knowledge Management (KM) initiatives, for example focusing on customer services and performance improvements. However, other countries have failed to realise the benefits that have been generated by implementing these successful KM initiatives.

The United Arab Emirates (UAE), a federal state established on 2 December 1971, consists of seven emirates. Each emirate enjoys broad independent political, judicial, financial and economic powers. The UAE constitution provides for the highest authority in the country to be the Supreme Council of Rulers of the seven emirates.

The UAE is one of the world's major producers of hydrocarbons. It has the seventh-largest global reserves of both crude oil and natural gas. Under current production rates, both reserves are expected to last more than 100 years (OPEC, 2014).

The Emirate of Abu Dhabi is the largest emirate in the federation, occupying over 86% of the country's total area. It is inhabited by more than 40% of the total population of the country. The emirate contributes about 57% of the total UAE Gross Domestic Product (GDP) (Abu Dhabi Council for Economic Development [ADCED], 2012) and accounts for more than 90% of crude oil and natural gas resources in the country (IMF, 2004). The Emirate of Dubai is the second largest, occupying about 5% of the country's total area. It contributes over one-quarter of the country's total GDP (Dubai Statistics Center, 2012; UAE National Bureau of Statistics, 2012). Dubai has developed considerable non-hydrocarbon activities—successfully contributing about 85% of the total UAE non-oil exports—followed by the Emirate of Abu Dhabi, with a contribution of 10% (International Monetary Fund [IMF], 2004). The other five emirates adopt a mixture of industrial and commercial activities, but they primarily rely on federal financial support and the support of the Emirates of Abu Dhabi and Dubai.

The UAE is a member state of the Gulf Cooperation Council (GCC). It has enjoyed impressive economic growth over the last few years, with a sustainable rise in the GDP per capita from US$28,100 in 1990 to US$39,100 in 2011. This growth apparently coincides with high oil revenues and high growth in the total labour force from 907,300 in 1990 to 6.2 million in 2012. These figures are dominated by foreign workers, with females representing about 15% (The World Bank Indicators: http://data.worldbank.org/indicator/). The local economy of the Emirate of Abu Dhabi is considerably stronger and has largely remained shockproof during the 2008 financial crisis, despite declining revenues from oil exports.

The country ranks within the top 40 countries in the latest Human Development Index (HDI), (third in the MENA region, after Saudi Arabia and Iran). Several scholars argue that such a good performance is a good indicator of a well-balanced and strong economy. However, the UAE faces a daunting challenge in diversifying its economy. According to 2012 statistics (OPEC, 2014), oil exports represented 31.9% of the country's GDP at 2013 current market prices, which is almost on par with Qatar (30.9%), but lower than other GCC countries who are members of OPEC (Saudi Arabia: 43.2%, Kuwait: 58.9%).

It is noteworthy that current diversification trends in the UAE are dictating a different pace across the different emirates that form the union. The Emirate of Dubai, for example, has succeeded in diversifying 90% of its economy away from hydrocarbons, while Abu Dhabi Emirate's economy is still 66% hydrocarbon-based (Wilson, 2010). The Abu Dhabi Emirate's desire to build a diversified economy, however, has prompted "The Abu Dhabi Economic Vision 2030". This long-term strategy, launched in 2009, seeks to reduce reliance on the hydrocarbon-based sector as a source of economic activity by increasing the contribution of non-hydrocarbon-based sectors to the emirate's GDP, focussing on knowledge-based industries in the future.

Despite the progress made towards economic diversification in most GCC countries, growth in the non-oil sector remained weak when compared to the growth of the domestic labour force. The heavy cost of diversification incurred by GCC countries, as indicated by Fasano and Iqbal (2003), amounted to heavy costs in terms of subsidies of power, water and credit, a lack or exemption of taxation and a heavy reliance on imported capital equipment and expatriate workers. The process, according to Fasano and Iqbal, has also involved a questionable partial transfer of oil wealth from the governments to citizens. The consequent ramifications of these policies led to the emergence of the GCC governments as the main investors in the economy, paying for most of the employment costs of the indigenous population. Further negative implications were marked by rising inflation and land prices in a real estate market developed in a disorderly manner. Provision of almost-free or highly subsidised energy—particularly water and electricity—in the presence of high demand and consumption (World Bank, 2005a) negatively impacted the sustainability of the energy industry due to its reliance on fluctuating government funds and spending.

In addition to several noticeable initiatives towards creating sustainable employment opportunities for nationals, the UAE has recently embarked on genuine diversification moves intended to reduce dependency on hydrocarbons and achieve the transition to a Knowledge Economy (KE). This process involves raising awareness about the fundamental concepts of KE across the private and public sectors, in line with the UAE Vision 2021 and the Federal Strategy 2011–2013. The strategy advocates for increasing investment in Science, Technology and Innovation (STI) and promotes Research and Development (R&D) with the aim of turning the economy into a KE. Countries that have substantially invested in knowledge components over the past few decades, such as Singapore and the Republic of Korea, have experienced rapid and sustained economic growth. These countries are currently among the most dynamic and competitive economies in the world; ranked second and 26th respectively according to the GCI for 2014–2015.

Realising the wide knowledge gap between the GCC countries—including the UAE, and the developed world in the West and Asia—and not only high growth and high returns but also stability and sustainability, are vital for economic development. Almost all GCC members are attempting a diversification route that underscores knowledge as the driving force in economic activities. By moving to innovation and KE, the UAE can reap huge benefits, including sustainable economic growth as a result of the expected increase of revenues from enhanced, high-quality exports and services that can compete in the global market. The country could thus achieve more diversification and reduce dependency on limited-production sectors, leading to a more stable economy and a better quality of life. Other envisaged KE benefits include the pivotal role that the KE might play in strengthening socio-political stability and enhancing productivity as a result of injecting new skills into the labour force.

UAE WORKFORCE

Similar to other Arab countries in the Gulf region, the social systems in the UAE are derived from core values, ethics and behaviours originated from Islam. Quranic principles and the teachings of the Prophet Mohammad serve as a religious and cultural habitat that guides individuals in conducting their daily activities (for more discussion, see Mellahi, 2003; Smith, 2006; Schlumberger, 2000).

Ali (1996) stresses that Islam is one of the most influential forces in the Arab World; moulding and regulating individual and group behaviour and outlooks. Islamic and Bedouin values and traditions are therefore the core components of the Arabic social system, which differ vastly from the cultural values and social attitudes in the rest of the world. Furthermore, Islamic values and teaching place a strong emphasis on obedience to leaders, who considerably influence the lives of not only the residents, but also the way businesses operate in the UAE. In addition to Islamic teaching, tribal and family traditions have a strong impact on individual behaviour.

The rate of change in the UAE has been perhaps one of the fastest in the world. This has led to unique social, political and human resources issues in the country, as economic growth has affected all spheres of life. High dependence on an expatriate workforce has been one of the unintended consequences of the socio-economic changes in the UAE. According to the UAE National Bureau of Statistics report (2012), UAE's population has been growing at an average rate of 6.3% per year for the last few decades, resulting in an increase from just 1 million in 1980 to at least 6.2 million in 2007. In 2010, the population jumped to 8.3 million, out of which 7.3 million are expatriates and less than 1 million are UAE nationals. In fact, based on 2010 estimates, the UAE nationals comprise only about 12%—around 947,997 of the total UAE population.

The public service authorities in the UAE continuously focus on improving services but are naturally faced with a number of challenges, essentially arising from UAE's distinct work environment. These unique challenges include the impact of strong religious values on legislation and governance structures, the under-representation of females and nationals in the workforce, and a population with a vast majority of foreign immigrants bringing their own different social, cultural and religious values into the country.

PURPOSE OF THE BOOK

The UAE government envisages being a world-class government by providing its citizens with the best access to knowledge and services in the most efficient, effective and economic way. In support of this vision, the UAE government has placed considerable focus on a comprehensive strategic planning exercise to transform the country's economic structure from relying heavily on hydrocarbon resources to becoming a knowledge-based economy.

The main objectives of this book are:

- Using empirical analysis to evaluate the extent of the UAE's success in diversifying its economy and utilising knowledge.
- Exploring the role of STI in transforming the UAE into a KE. Further evaluating the country's STI capacity and competence in exercising adoption and diffusion of knowledge.
- Evaluating UAE's performance in terms of global competitiveness and technological readiness.
- Assessing UAE's achievements in implementing the KE pillars to transform its economy into a sustainable knowledge-based economy.

Throughout the book, a number of key issues facing the UAE in transforming its economy to a knowledge-based economy will be critically analysed and discussed.

APPROACH OF THE BOOK

For the purpose of this book, several sources have been reviewed and consulted. Information was located via searchable databases from various universities (such as Sussex and Brighton in the UK and UAEU in UAE), from different mainstream refereed journals (focusing on KM, knowledge-based economy, economics, development economies, change management, management, HR, social science, strategy, etc.), as well as books, online databases, governmental reports and statistics.

The first few chapters will provide details of the aims and objectives of the research, as well as reviewing some of the literature and theories on KM, knowledge-based economy and sustainable economic development models and frameworks in the context of the UAE.

In Chapter 4, the research methods and data used to realise each of the research objectives of the study will be detailed. We will be using a deductive approach in order to explore existing data and test theories through primary research. The study will employ a mixed research methodology, where both quantitative and qualitative means will be used to analyse collected data.

The focus of Chapter 5 is to empirically evaluate the extent of the UAE's success in diversifying its economy and utilising knowledge and available technological infrastructures in domesticating the manufacture and production of technology products as important sources of wealth generation. The chapter will therefore provide a strong case for diversifying the UAE's economy and implementing the principles and approaches of KE in the country.

Chapter 6 aims to explore the role of STI in transforming the UAE into a KE by initially assessing the country's achievements in implementing the KE pillars. It further evaluates the country's STI capacity and competence in exercising the adoption and diffusion of knowledge.

The main objective of Chapter 7 is to assess and evaluate the UAE's performance in terms of global competitiveness and technological readiness. In this chapter we have taken a somewhat extensive review of the different aspects of technology (products, transfer, ICTs, etc.) in the UAE. This chapter will also aim to identify the opportunities and challenges of ICTs and education for improving the technological readiness in the UAE.

Chapter 8 provides a clear road map towards a sustainable knowledge-based economy in the UAE by outlining the key success factors that ensure the sustainability of any knowledge-based initiatives and practices within the UAE.

Finally, in Chapter 9, we will feature a detailed case study about the Abu Dhabi Government (ADG) Department of Municipal Affairs (DMA) Major Knowledge Management Project—Musharaka, which is considered the first transformation project of its kind, changing employees' culture in the government of Abu Dhabi.

2

CHAPTER

LITERATURE REVIEW

WASD

INTRODUCTION

This chapter will serve as the initial step in investigating the research objectives of this study by reviewing the extant literature—both in theory as well as practice—on subjects including Knowledge Management (KM) and sustainable economic development models and frameworks within the context of the UAE.

We aim to provide an in-depth and critical review of the literature and theories about knowledge and KM, as well as the concepts and approaches relating to the Knowledge-based Economy (KE). In doing so, several sources have been reviewed and consulted (including management, human resources management, social science, strategy, science, technology, innovation, etc.), as well as books, online databases, governmental reports and statistics.

We will also critically analyse various international cases of organisations that have undertaken major KM transformation projects within their boundaries. Therefore, our ultimate aim is to ensure a strong case for implementing the principles of KE and securing the necessary leadership buy-in from the early stages of the transformation process.

ORGANISATIONAL LEARNING VERSUS LEARNING ORGANISATION

In his famous book, *The Age of Unreason*, Handy (1989) argues that the world of work is changing because the organisations of work are changing. At the same time, however, organisations are having to adapt to a changing world of work. Moreover, in the future, he argues that organisations will be knowledge-based, run by a few smart people and populated by a host of smart machines.

Huber (1991, p.89) argues that an entity learns if, through its processing of information, the range of its potential behaviour is changed. Organisational learning is a concept used to describe certain types of activity that take place in an organisation, and therefore a learning organisation is one that is good at organisational learning (see Tsang, 1997, p.74).

According to Probst and Buchel (1997, p.15), organisational learning is the process by which the organisation's knowledge and value base changes, leading to improved problem-solving ability and capacity for action. Organisational learning occurs through shared insight, knowledge and mental models, and builds on past knowledge and experience; that is, on memory (Stata, 1989, p.64).

A learning organisation is an organisation skilled at creating, acquiring and transferring knowledge and modifying behaviour to reflect new knowledge and insights (Garvin, 1993, p.80). For Fiol and Lyles (1985, p.803), organisational learning means the process of improving actions through better knowledge and understanding.

WHAT IS 'KNOWLEDGE'?

There is a large amount of literature about knowledge with different views and opinions (Alavi and Leidner, 1999, 2001; Holsapple and Joshi, 2002; Joshi et al., 2007; Kettinger and Li, 2010; McQueen, 1998; Nonaka, 1994; Zack, 1999a, 1999b). However, the nature of knowledge and defining knowledge is not a simple undertaking (Purvis et al., 2001).

According to Gebba (2013), knowledge first began with the ancient Egyptians, Greeks and Romans, who developed several mechanisms to record and transfer knowledge to following generations. Al-Yahya and Farah (2009) characterised knowledge as "intangible and difficult to measure; volatile; predominantly embedded in people's minds; not consumable and can increase over time; it can have a variety of impacts within organisations; it cannot be bought, as it accumulates over time; and it can be used by different processes at the same time". For Drucker (1998), knowledge is simply information that changes something or somebody: either by becoming grounds for action or by making an individual (or an institution) capable of different or more effective action. This definition addresses both the individual and corporate aspects of knowledge.

However, from a management perspective, Nonaka and Takeuchi (1995) argue that the key difference between information and knowledge is that information is much more easily identified, organised and distributed. Knowledge, on the other hand, cannot really be managed because it resides in one's mind. While there are various typologies, in its simplest form there are two main types of knowledge—tacit and explicit. Explicit knowledge may be expressed and communicated relatively easily; tacit knowledge tends to be personal, subjective and difficult to transmit (or sometimes even to recognise). Thus, while some explicit knowledge may lend itself to codification and commodification in Knowledge Management Systems (KMS), tacit knowledge is very strongly embedded within the mind of the individual and is highly context-sensitive (Barnes, 2002). Alavi and Leidner (2001) define KMS as a class of information system applied to managing organisational knowledge. A key challenge of KMS, therefore, has been to make appropriate tacit knowledge explicit and portable (Swan, 2001).

WHY MANAGING KNOWLEDGE?

Knowledge and KM have attracted immense attention in academia, with great interest being seen in economics, management, information technology, anthropology, sociology, epistemology, psychology and other disciplines (Quintas et al., 1997). Several notable scholars have long argued that the long-term prosperity of many organisations depends on the organisational effort to explicitly manage the knowledge of their employees and use it as a source for growth and corporate profit (Haslinda and Sarinah, 2009; Herschel and Nemati, 2000; Herschel et al., 2001). Skyrme and Amidon (1998) argue that KM has become a core competence that companies must develop in order to succeed in tomorrow's dynamic global economy.

In recent years, a substantial amount of literature has been written about the role knowledge and KM play in organisational excellence and in building an enabling environment to foster economic growth and promote the knowledge economy (see Ahmed, 2005; Ahmed and Al-Roubaie, 2012; Danofsky, 2005; Hamel, 2005; Mansell and Wehn, 1998).

Many scholars argue that the main purpose for organisations to adopt KM is to create a common space for individuals to interact for the exchange and creation of knowledge (see Alavi and Leidner, 2001; Ahn and Chang, 2004; De Pablos, 2002; Margaryan et al., 2011).

Knowledge is a critical success factor for organisations, particularly in the long term (Mansell and Wehn, 1998; Stewart, 2001; Tat and Hase, 2007) and knowledge is more likely to be the only resource within organisations that is hard for rivals to copy (Nonaka and Takeuchi, 1995).

In order for organisations to be successful in today's business environment, KM has become an important area of focus for many of them (Yelden and Albers, 2004). Therefore, utilising knowledge resources effectively and efficiently appears to be a pivotal factor in obtaining a competitive advantage and ensuring Sustainable Development (SD) for both societies and organisations (Davenport and Prusak, 1998; Nonaka, 1998; Storey and Barnett, 2000).

Hamel (2005) and Juma (2003) argue that knowledge is the chief currency and the essence of the modern age; it can also be a strategic resource and a lifeline for Developing Countries' (DCs) SD. Therefore, all nations, particularly those with limited natural resources and inadequate financial endowments, can benefit from the new economy by investing in knowledge creation and information dissemination. Knowledge has not only become an important factor input, but also a major source of employment and wealth creation. Thus, investment in human capital provides an economy with an excellent opportunity to diversify production and sustain growth.

Moreover, for Cao et al. (2013) knowledge is a powerful resource in helping both organisations and individuals preserve their identity, culture, best practices and core competencies. However, far from focusing simply on the processes of sharing and disseminating knowledge, the emphasis should also be on the importance of generating home-grown knowledge as a potentially powerful tool in development strategies. Sharing experiences among practitioners, putting into practice the latest research and techniques, learning from the latest life-saving techniques, combining local and global practices – these are powerful reminders of how KM is having a major impact on health.

Beazley et al. (2002) argue that the typical productivity cost of an employee leaving an organisation is 85% of their base salary, due to their replacement's mistakes, lost knowledge and lost skills. Moreover, the results of several surveys reveal that 87% of European business directors believe they could enhance their company's competitiveness with improved KM and 76% believe that building and sharing knowledge is important for their company (see Williams, 2003).

The case of the Severe Acute Respiratory Syndrome (SARS) epidemic is a good example of how knowledge sharing can accelerate development in science and benefit people. During this epidemic, the Human Genome Project data was made available to scientists to turn a collection of individual sequences into an incomparably richer resource (see PLoS for more details). The timely availability, reliability and usability of information not only averts epidemic diseases, but also leads to prevention that improves people's health. Moreover, knowledge or evidence-based policymaking is indispensable if gaps in living standards are to be narrowed.

Wild and Laumer (2011) argue that the success of KM is defined through the acceptance and usage of KMS, while Zack (1999a, 1999b) states that the success of KM initiatives requires organisations to understand their knowledge requirements and implement appropriate technologies to meet their knowledge-processing needs. However, Zyngier and Burstein (2004) argue that the successful implementation of KM in organisations requires the development of a systematic and deliberate KM strategy, referring to identifying areas in which knowledge is critical and setting up the actions, tools and methods that can best leverage knowledge.

In a highly cited article referencing the work of the IBM Institute for Knowledge-Based Organisations with leading companies and government organisations, Fontaine and Lesser (2002) outline various challenges facing organisations when implementing KM. These challenges represent major barriers that hinder the successful implementation of KM within these organisations, costing time, money and resources, and therefore not producing good results. These barriers include:

- Failure to align KM efforts with the organisation's strategic objectives.
- Creation of repositories without addressing the need to manage content.
- Failure to understand and connect KM into individuals' daily work activities.
- An overemphasis on formal learning efforts as a mechanism for sharing knowledge.
- Focusing KM efforts only within organisational boundaries.

KM MODELS AND FRAMEWORKS

In their famous ground paper entitled Perspectives on knowledge management models, Cristea and Capatina (2009) analysed three key models and frameworks for KM, namely: von Krogh and Roos, Nonaka/Takeuchi, Wiig, Boisot and Bennet. In their comprehensive analysis of these KM models, Cristea and Capatina describe the most important characteristics, the main factors involved and the different types of knowledge and elements forming each model. Furthermore, Cristea and Capatina provide comments about the advantages and disadvantages of each model, as well as their usefulness in the economic environment.

In another similar famous review of KM models, Haslinda and Sarinah (2009) critically review the various KM models: Boisot; Hedlund and Nonaka; Skandia Intellectual Capital; Demerest; Frid; Kogut and Zander; as well as Stankosky and Baldanza's KM Framework. The review reveals that these various KM models vary in perspectives, ranging from the basic assumption of the articulation and transfer of tacit and explicit knowledge to the more complex and complicated assumption that knowledge is intellectual capital, which is mechanistic in perspective as well as an important asset that has to be managed efficiently for a firm's success. Haslinda and Sarinah argue that these models have their own way of placing the major KM activities and enablers, with the aim of producing a dynamic system to reinforce the organisation's core competencies. Moreover, the KM process is the action step that an organisation uses to identify its needs and the manner in which it collects, adapts and transfers that information across the organisation. Through the KM process, the models can be used to foster the development of organisational knowledge and enhance the impact of individuals throughout the organisation.

Yang et al. (2009) critically evaluate selected KM models and propose a holistic KM model. The authors argue that most existing KM models tend to narrowly define knowledge from conceptual and perceptual perspectives and fail to recognise affectual knowledge, such as values and visions. Yang et al. also argue that most KM models view KM as a linear or cyclical process and thus fail to identify the multidimensional nature of the knowledge dynamics between individuals and organisations.

Peter Heisig's (2009) article, Harmonisation of knowledge management—comparing 160 KM frameworks around the globe, is claimed to be the first quantitative and qualitative analysis of 160 KM frameworks from different origins worldwide. In his study, aiming to discover the differences and correspondences of KM frameworks, Heisig analysed the elements of 160 KM frameworks from research and practice collected worldwide. However despite the wide range of terms used in the KM frameworks, Heisig's study reveals that an underlying consensus was detected regarding the basic categories used to describe the KM activities and critical success factors. Moreover Heisig, similar to other scholars mentioned above, noted that there is still a need to develop an improved understanding in research and practice with regard to the core term knowledge.

Table 2.1 below includes the major KM models and frameworks analysed and discussed by key studies and research, with a common description of these models and frameworks.

Table 2.1 Analysis of KM models and frameworks	
KM Models/Frameworks	*Description*
Krogh and Roos	Based on an epistemological approach that knowledge is found both in the individual mind and in the relations between people.
Nonaka and Takeuchi	The central argument of the model is the transformation of tacit knowledge into explicit knowledge (knowledge spiral) as the essential base for learning and innovation at individual, group and organisational levels.
Hedlund and Nonaka	KM is seen from the categorical view in which knowledge is categorised into discrete elements, to the more complicated and complex perspective of knowledge that is mechanistic and socially constructed orientation.
Wiig	In order to ensure perspectives and purposes, Wiig's main claim is that knowledge can only be useful when it is organised using semantic networks.
Choo	Analyses how informational elements are found in organisational actions.
Skandia Intellectual Capital	Assumes that intellectual capital are vital assets in organisation and should be managed efficiently for a firm's success.
Demerest	Intrinsically linked with the social and learning process within organisations.
Frid	Suggests that knowledge should be managed systematically and of equal emphasis at all KM process levels.
Stankosky and Baldanza	Emphasise that leadership, organisation structure, technology infrastructure and learning are important foundations for KM in an organisation.
Kogut and Zander	Focus on the strategic importance of knowledge as a source of competitive advantage.
Adaptive Models	Very well suited for modelling KM processes by treating the organisation as a living organism concerned with an independent existence, which is concerned with its surviving at almost any moment.

KM CASE STUDIES

In this part of the chapter, we will critically analyse various international case studies from a number of organisations that have undertaken major KM transformation projects within their boundaries. In addition to providing a brief critical observation from each case study and identifying the various elements from the case that are relevant to UAE, there will also be a focus on the practice and challenges of KM within various international organisations.

Table 2.2	Sustaining human capital in the US Federal Agencies	CASE STUDY
Organisation overview	The USA has a large number of government organisations that operate at the federal level. These organisations work within domains that cater for areas of interest to the entire American nation, such as forest protection, national security, the space programme, etc.	
Case study	The need for government-wide KM has been triggered by the fact that a very large proportion of federal civil servants are due to retire within the next few years. The know-how in many of the federal agencies will become at risk due to the lack of formal mechanisms to capture, share, apply and leverage knowledge.	
	A number of agencies have followed a KM Pyramid model (framework), which was based on people, processes and technology. The Pyramid also focuses on generating and sharing knowledge both internally and externally, in addition to linking KM to human capital to assure the sustainability of the vital workforce. The KM Pyramid has a two-year rollout plan. The first year focusses on awareness, technology infrastructure and quick wins, while the second year focusses on formal rollout and change management and setting up the permanent organisation units and roles to assure the sustainability of KM activities.	
	The investment in KM has enabled the US federal government to continuously build the workforce for the future.	
Observations	The general approach and structure of the KM Pyramid has helped a number of government organisations to introduce the KM concepts. However the two-year rollout plan might not be sufficient for the various organisations.	
	Delivering a fit-for-purpose KM framework is a key factor for success; therefore the Pyramid model lacks the mechanism and guidance for selecting the appropriate KM components based on the organisation's strategy. The content and duration of the rollout plan should be tailored based on organisation specific needs and readiness for change.	
KM components	Shadowing, Job Rotation, Lessons Learned, Communities.	
Reference	Liebowitz (2003).	

Table 2.3	Global KM system in Accenture	
Organisation overview	Accenture is the world's largest consulting firm with multinational management consulting and technology services. The firm has over 260,000 employees, globally delivering on the front end of many industries.	
Case study	Accenture was among the first organisations that deployed KM on a global scale, with spending exceeding $500 million. The organisation aimed to support knowledge sharing between consultants throughout the various consultancy projects. At the centre of the KM efforts, Accenture has developed a sophisticated IT system called Knowledge Exchange (KX). The system contains materials extracted from the deliverables to the clients globally, such as presentations, best practices and proposals. KX has enabled employees to access key materials to support them throughout the delivery phases of client engagements. However, the full potential utilisation of the system was limited by the lack of utilisation of knowledge from certain geographical areas.	
Observations	Accenture's approach to KM has been influenced by the technology nature of the company, which resulted in a system that supports the content management side of the KM but not the collaboration aspects. KM technology should be defined based on an integrated KM framework of people and processes. It is also critical to align the KM Framework with the local strategy.	
KM components	Knowledge Assets Management, Knowledge Classification and Find-ability.	
Reference	Yongsun and Choi (2005).	

Table 2.4	Communities of Practice (CoPs) in the Centres for Disease Control and Prevention	
Organisation overview	The Centres for Disease Control and Prevention (CDC) is a federal institute that looks after public health issues in the USA. The CDC focuses on enhancing the national health through giving attention to matters related to the control and prevention of diseases.	
Case study	CoPs have been used as a medium for collaboration and knowledge sharing within CDC, and externally with a number of stakeholders within the healthcare domain. A number of communities have been formed with goals and objectives to enhance sharing in a number of clinical areas. CDC has benefited greatly from the rollout of CoPs in enhancing the KX between healthcare professionals; the initiative also supported relationships across the healthcare domains. CoPs have helped CDC and others within the healthcare industry to enhance their performance and ultimately save lives.	
Observations	CDC and other healthcare organisations could further enhance CoPs by providing a common operational framework supported by tools and technologies to manage the CoPs. Another improvement might be introduced by human resources to formally dedicate time for CoPs participation so it does not become a burden on the busy healthcare professionals.	
KM components	Communities.	
References	http://www.cdc.gov/ Mabery et al. (2013).	

Table 2.5 Multilingual KMS in the Food and Agriculture Organization of the United Nations (FAO)		CASE STUDY
Organisation overview	The FAO is an agency of the United Nations with local offices in more than 80 countries. It is mandated with increasing agricultural productivity, improving nutrition, raising the standard of living in rural communities and contributing to global economic growth.	
Case study	The FAO disseminates key knowledge to their stakeholders, primarily via the World Agriculture Information Centre (WAICENT). It has multiple resources for key knowledge.	
	Due to the global nature of the FAO, the various resources tend to be in multiple languages and are not available most of the time in all the languages supported via WAICENT portal.	
	The WAICENT portal provides connections between similar content in different languages. This capability is delivered via the utilisation of a common information taxonomy that links the various languages via a structuring of the taxonomy to support conversions, content and connections.	
	On the technology side, the portal utilises XML technology to effectively manage and provide the basis for governing the content structure, making it ready for presentation in the appropriate language interface.	
	The WAICENT portal played a vital role in disseminating key information from the FAO to their stakeholders around the globe: information dissemination is a key pillar for enabling FAO to deliver its mandate.	
Observations	The KM system in the FAO is more an information management initiative than a KM framework. Information management is a key aspect of KM, but it does not assure full management of the knowledge cycle through the organisation.	
	Technology and information are important aspects of KM, however people and processes are needed for a full KM framework.	
KM components	Taxonomy.	
Reference	O'Leary (2008).	

Table 2.6	Knowledge sharing culture in Sarkuysan 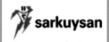
Organisation overview	Founded in 1972, Sarkuysan is the first publicly owned company in Turkey and specialises in producing electrolytic copper products. Sarkuysan has a production capacity of over 200,000 tonnes and supplies key materials for several industries, including power generation, electronics, automotive and communication.
Case study	KM practices at Sarkuysan are focussed on story telling that forms a strong part of the organisation's culture; this is supported by the top management team. Employees have easy access to the top management; sharing of ideas and suggestions for improvements are encouraged and rewarded via a formal reward structure. Knowledge sharing is also supported by several cultural factors, such as corporate citizenship and team spirit. KM activities and culture at Sarkuysan have helped the company to utilise the tacit knowledge among the employees, which, in turn, contributed to the unprecedented success throughout the years.
Observations	A management support and rewards scheme is a key factor in the success of the knowledge sharing activities within Sarkuysan. Sarkuysan would benefit from the introduction of other KM aspects; the current company culture would set the foundation for an integrated KM framework to further support the company culture.
KM components	Suggestions Scheme, Lessons Learned, KM Strategy.
References	Nayir and Uzunçarsili (2008) http://www.sarkuysan.com/en-EN/about-us/119.aspx.

Table 2.7	Starbucks and customer knowledge
Organisation overview	Starbucks is the largest coffee house company in the world, with over 18,000 stores in 62 countries.
Case study	The company's financial performance in 2008 flagged the need to establish a closer relationship with customers. The company decided to use social media as platform for sharing information with their customers, receiving information/suggestions from their customers and collecting information about their customers. Starbucks has utilised the following media channels for their customers' KM: *Twitter*: Pushing information about their latest products and events and collecting suggestions and concerns. *Facebook*: Establishing an online community of loyal customers and facilitating KX. *Foursquare*: Providing day-to-day updates and collecting tips andsuggestions from customers. *MyStarbucksIdea*: Collecting new ideas by customers and reviewing progress by Starbucks. The four channels work together to support customer-centric development of products, allowing the company to deliver fit-for-purpose products.
Observations	Effective KX via social media has enabled Starbucks to provide fit-for-purpose products and promote its brand, which has, in turn, supported business growth.
KM components	Communities, Suggestions Scheme.
References	Chua and Banerjee (2013) http://www.starbucks.com/ http://www.facebook.com/Starbucks.

Table 2.8	**CoPs in the United States Agency for International Development (USAID)** CASE STUDY

Organisation overview	USAID is a federal US agency responsible for managing civilian foreign aid on behalf of the US government. The organisation was formed in 1961 under the Kennedy administration to implement government aid in the areas pre-approved by Congress.
Case study	USAID has a KM programme under the Chief Information Officer. The programme aims to promote and support knowledge sharing activities throughout the organisation. The organisation has a framework that supports the knowledge cycle through the phases of generate, capture, share and apply.
	Among the key initiatives adopted by the USAID and the Global Alliance for Pre-Service Education (GAPS), CoPs was implemented to act as an interface to connect people from DCs.
	Each one of the CoPs focuses on a particular health issue/domain. The CoPs operated as virtual communities online and this has enabled CoPs to reach a good number of individuals all over the world to share their expertise, challenges and issues.
	Despite the success of CoPs, the quality of Internet connectivity and access restrictions limited the utilisation of the planned benefits in a number of DCs.
Observations	CoPs deployed by USAID has improved KX in key health areas and ultimately saved lives. More integration between CoPs and the wider KM activities in USAID would introduce added-value in the form of more effective knowledge sharing across the various stakeholders.
	A holistic approach for KM would assure that the entire organisation works collectively to achieve the organisation's goals; this could be achieved via the integration of the current front end KX channels with an internal KM framework.
KM components	Communities.
References	Thomas et al. (2010) http://www.usaid.gov/results-and-data/information-resources/knowledge-management-support.

Table 2.9 Enhancing customer services at Tehran Municipality	CASE STUDY

Organisation overview	Tehran Municipality provides a number of municipal services to the city and is led by Tehran's Mayor. The municipality is supported by the Municipal Council (Showra), which has municipal legislative power.
	The Municipality is divided into 22 districts, with each district led by a mayor. The district offices carry out the administrative work in their areas.
Case study	Tehran municipality operates a customer facing process (process 137) that handles citizens' complaints, issues and suggestions. The clerks at the municipality receive calls from citizens and each call could be related to any one of the 620 kinds of city problems.
	The process is fairly knowledge-intensive and each resolution might involve one or more of the municipality's departments.
	The improvement work at the municipality has utilised TQM approaches and looked into individual activities with a focus on knowledge needs. The scope covered aspects such as creation storage, sharing and applying.
	The process has been reengineered to assure an effective flow of information through various activities and across departments involved in the execution of process 137. This work assured the delivery of the right information to the right people at the right time.
	Tehran municipality has successfully enhanced its performance in serving the citizens via the effective management of process 137 knowledge facets.
Observations	The work at Tehran Municipality is an excellent example of aligning KM with quality management and business process management to produce added-value and enhance organisational performance.
	Applying the same to the internal processes would further enhance the internal work within the municipality.
KM components	KM Strategy, Taxonomy.
References	Ranjbarfard et al. (2013). http://en.tehran.ir/.

In concluding this part of the chapter, it is evident from the literature review that knowledge is intangible and is the reason why many organisations find it difficult to see a clear business outcome from any KM processes and activities. And despite the importance of KM for various organisations, senior executives continuously ask for justification for any investment in KM initiatives within their organisations. The models reviewed are found to have various KM processes fostering the development of organisation knowledge and consequently achieving excellence.

3

CHAPTER

MAKING THE CASE FOR THE KNOWLEDGE-BASED ECONOMY

INTRODUCTION

...Our mission is to establish the UK as a leading knowledge economy... our objective in policy must be to create a successful, knowledge-based economy which rests on innovation and a highly skilled labour force. That is what my own job is about.

A speech entitled "Innovation and the UK's Knowledge Economy" by Dr. Vince Cable, the former UK Secretary of State for Business, Innovation and Skills, 22 July 2014, London, UK.

WHAT IS THE 'KNOWLEDGE-BASED ECONOMY'?

Many scholars argue that information can lead to knowledge, and knowledge is a prerequisite for development (see Ahmed, 2005; Ahmed and Al-Roubaie, 2012; Ahmed and Nwagwu, 2006; Danofsky, 2005; Hamel, 2005; Mansell and Wehn, 1998; World Bank, 2008, 2012; United Nations including UNDP, various years; etc.). In this regard, the Organisation for Economic Co-operation and Development (OECD, 1997) has underscored that "knowledge and information tend to be abundant; what is scarce is the capacity to use them in meaningful ways". Moreover UNESCO's 32nd General Conference in 2003 focussed on "Building knowledge societies and advancement of knowledge-based practices" as an essential component of globalisation and sustainable economic growth, particularly in DCs.

The socio-economic, industrial, technological and cultural transformations over the years have led to what is currently known as the "knowledge society" (Wiig, 1997). However, in the last 20 years, knowledge assets have often become more important to companies than financial and physical assets, and are often the only way for a company to distinguish itself from its competitors and gain a competitive advantage (Yelden and Albers, 2004). Therefore, over the last few years, we have witnessed the emergence of what has increasingly become a KE society.

The concept of a KE is used to describe an economy that creates, disseminates and uses knowledge to enhance its growth and development. According to various reports by the World Bank (2008, 2012), a successful KE is characterised by close links between academic science and industrial technology. This is empowered by increased education and lifelong learning, and greater investment in intangibles such as Research and Development (R&D) and software. It places a greater importance on innovation for economic growth and competitiveness than a non-KE. The application of knowledge in the economy implies an efficient means of production and delivery of goods and services at lower costs to a greater population size. Therefore, the application of knowledge in economic development entails investing in strategies that produce significant changes in the way a country can grow (Salmi, 2009).

In line with the economic theory relating to knowledge economies, the Global Competitiveness Index (GCI) (GC Report, 2011–2012) assumes three stages in an economic development and competitiveness path. The first stage—the factor-driven stage—entails competition between countries based on their endowments and natural resources. This is driven by well-functioning institutions, a well-developed infrastructure and the provision of at least basic education to a healthy workforce. The transition into the second stage—the efficiency-driven stage—develops as the country entertains increased productivity and competitiveness. In this stage, efficient production processes and product quality are needed. Factors influencing this stage include investment in higher education, the provision of training for the workforce and the ability to harness the benefits of existing technologies. At the last development stage—the innovation-driven stage—countries are expected to compete by producing new and different goods using the most sophisticated production processes and by innovating new processes and goods (GC Report, 2011–2012). Innovation implies sufficient domestic manufacturing, the production of technology products and equipment catering to domestic needs, and an increase of access to imports and exports in international markets.

The knowledge economy fostering growth in modern economies is not possible without knowledge creation and technological diffusion. In the new economy, balanced and sustainable economic development stems from the production and export of high-tech products and services for global markets. Participating in global trade and finance requires countries to build an enabling environment capable of enhancing competitiveness, increasing linkages, encouraging technology transfer, promoting innovation, disseminating information, acquiring skills and absorbing knowledge.

Knowledge economies produce, distribute and create knowledge. Important features of the knowledge economy are growth in technological diffusion, skills acquisition and lifelong learning—used to produce knowledge intensity products and creative ideas to foster rapid economic growth and SD. Knowledge has become an important input, not only in job creation, but also in economic diversification and wealth creation. It is not possible for an economy to compete and gain global access without knowledge support systems based on production and distribution of knowledge and technology.

A KE revolves around investment in R&D, and in innovation as the basis for the capacity building necessary for knowledge absorption and information dissemination. Technological diffusion involves technological learning, in which knowledge workers augment their capabilities to absorb and adapt knowledge. Universities and training centres should adopt programmes that upgrade skill levels of workers—in turn, enhancing the economy's ability to distribute and share knowledge.

Acknowledging the importance of knowledge for long-term economic growth, the World Bank introduced the KE framework. This asserted that sustained investments in education, innovation, ICTs and the creation of a conducive economic institutional environment would lead to increases in the use and creation of knowledge in economic production, subsequently resulting in sustained economic growth (Chen and Dahlman, 2006). The framework constitutes the following four pillars as necessary for the realisation of the KE factors in a country:

- An economic and institutional regime to provide incentives for the efficient use of existing and new knowledge, and the flourishing of entrepreneurship.
- An educated and skilled population to create, share and use knowledge well.
- An efficient innovation system of firms, research centres, universities, consultants and other organisations to tap into the growing stock of global knowledge, assimilate and adapt it to local needs, and create new technology.
- ICT to facilitate the effective creation, dissemination and processing of information.

In this context, the World Bank Knowledge Assessment Methodology (KAM) (www.worldbank. org/kam) is utilised to provide an overview of all countries' performance worldwide, based on the four pillars of KE. Eventually, the World Bank's Knowledge Economy Index (KEI) and

Knowledge Index (KI) are deployed to gauge the conduciveness of the country's environment for an effective use of knowledge in the economic development process, and to assess the country's competence in exercising the adoption and diffusion of knowledge.

Using KAM (www.worldbank.org/kam), the recent performance of all countries (146) is illustrated in Table 3.1. These indexes reflect the readiness of world economies to take advantage of the new economy and speed up the process of economic transformation. The picture across most counties varies from economies with impressive progress towards knowledge-based economies and building capacity for knowledge creation, such as Sweden (KEI = 9.43, KI = 9.38), to economies with a large decrease in their KEI, such as Myanmar (KEI = 0.96, KI = 1.22).

Table 3.1 World KEI and KI 2012				
Rank	Change	Country	KEI	KI
1	0	Sweden	9.43	9.38
2	6	Finland	9.33	9.22
3	0	Denmark	9.16	9.00
4	−2	Netherlands	9.11	9.22
5	2	Norway	9.11	8.99
6	3	New Zealand	8.97	8.93
7	3	Canada	8.92	8.72
8	7	Germany	8.9	8.83
9	−3	Australia	8.88	8.98
10	−5	Switzerland	8.87	8.65
145	−16	Myanmar	0.96	1.22
Regions				
1	0	North America	8.8	8.7
2	0	Europe and Central Asia	7.47	7.64
3	1	East Asia and the Pacific	5.32	5.17
4	1	Latin America	5.15	5.31
5	−2	World	5.12	5.01
6	0	Middle East and North Africa	4.74	4.51
7	1	South Asia	2.84	2.77
8	−1	Africa	2.55	2.43
Income Groups				
1	0	High Income	8.6	8.67
2	0	Upper Middle Income	5.1	5.07
3	0	Lower Middle Income	3.42	3.45
4	0	Low Income	1.58	1.58

Source: World Bank (2012).

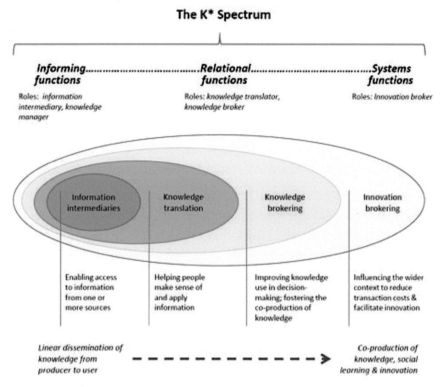

The K* Spectrum

Informing..Relational..Systems
functions   functions   functions

Roles: *information*   Roles: *knowledge translator,*   Roles: *Innovation broker*
intermediary, knowledge   *knowledge broker*
manager

Information intermediaries | Knowledge translation | Knowledge brokering | Innovation brokering

Enabling access to information from one or more sources | Helping people make sense of and apply information | Improving knowledge use in decision-making; fostering the co-production of knowledge | Influencing the wider context to reduce transaction costs & facilitate innovation

Linear dissemination of knowledge from producer to user — — — — — — — — — —▶ *Co-production of knowledge, social learning & innovation*

Source: Reproduced with permission of the authors from Shaxson et al. (2012). For a publication in submission by Shaxson et al.

Figure 3.1

**The K* Spectrum—there is a spectrum of knowledge sharing activities,
which are all systemically related to each other**

UNITED NATIONS UNIVERSITY K* (KSTAR) CONCEPT

From 25–27 April 2012, one of the authors (Allam Ahmed) participated in a landmark, invitation-only conference in Hamilton, Ontario, Canada, organised by Louise Shaxson[1] and Alex Bielak[2] under the aegis of the United Nations University. The conference was an excellent opportunity to meet and discuss various issues relating to KM with scholars and practitioners from across the world. Delegates at the conference discussed their understanding of KM together with other, more familiar terms, such as Knowledge Translation, KX, Knowledge Intermediation, Knowledge Brokering, Knowledge Mobilisation and others.

---

[1] Louise Shaxson is a senior Research Fellow at ODI. She has contributed to several ground-breaking publications including the *K* Concept Paper* and *Knowledge, Policy and Power in International Development: A Practical Guide* (The Policy Press).

[2] Dr. Alex Bielak is an internationally recognised Knowledge Translation and Brokering authority who has developed the K* (KStar) concept, bringing together experts in the field from different sectors worldwide for the first time, while serving as Senior Research Fellow and Knowledge Broker with the United Nations University Institute for Water, Environment and Health in Canada.

However, one of the many outcomes from the conference, which has been recently developed by Shaxson, Bielak and others, is the K* (KStar) Concept Paper, in which Shaxson et al. (2012), argue that:

> KM (is) the process of ensuring that knowledge is available. It is sometimes used to describe the suite of activities from the storage of information through to its dissemination. However, with the emergence of other terms and greater differentiation between roles, it is beginning to refer more to the collection and storage of different types of knowledge so that they can be accessed when needed.

As such, KM is a systemically related and critical element of the K* Spectrum (see Figure 3.1). It provides the solid informational foundations to facilitate efficient relational and systems functions, including knowledge and innovation brokering. Investing in such functions can lead to operational efficiencies, smoother, faster delivery and accelerated impact of various initiatives. However, as previously observed by Shaxson and Bielak, while many different organisations are looking at aspects of K* and placing increasing emphasis on KM and other K* activities, they are doing so in very different ways with diverse approaches, budgets and motivations.

CONCLUSIONS

It is evident from the literature review that knowledge is intangible and is the reason why many organisations find it difficult to see a clear business outcome from any KM processes and activities. Despite the importance of KM for various organisations, senior executives continuously ask for justification for any investment in KM initiatives within their organisations.

4

CHAPTER

METHODOLOGIES AND APPROACHES

WASD

INTRODUCTION

The aim of this chapter is to present research methodologies, including data and data sources, together with the analysis techniques used to investigate several research objectives in this book. The objectives are summarised as follows: first, assessing the UAE diversification level towards manufacturing sectors, away from the oil and gas sector. Second, evaluating the extent of success the UAE achieved in utilising knowledge and available technological infrastructure to move towards a Knowledge Economy (KE). Third, describing the UAE's position in terms of transition to a KE and global competitiveness; highlighting weaknesses, strengths and opportunities, in addition to exploring the role of Science, Technology and Innovation (STI) in transforming the country into a KE. Several sources have been consulted, including refereed journals, online databases, and governmental reports and statistics. In reviewing this literature, we will be using a deductive approach in order to explore existing data and test theories through primary research. By adopting an analytical and critical approach, we will be able to propose several relationships found between existing theories and primary research. The study will employ a mixed research methodology where both quantitative and qualitative means will be used to analyse collected data and information. In the following sections, research data and methods used to realise each of the above-mentioned research objectives are detailed.

FIRST: ECONOMIC DIVERSIFICATION

The assessment of the country's diversification towards manufacturing sectors is based on annual data from the UAE Bureau of Statistics National Accounts estimates. These cover the 1975–2010 period, representing both real UAE oil Gross Domestic Product (GDP) and manufacturing sector GDP, measured annually in the local UAE currency at 2001 constant prices.

The assessment of diversification is approached by utilising synchronisation techniques, which are usually used to measure the convergence or divergence of global business cycles—periodic irregular up-and-down movements in economic activities (see Mink et al., 2007). Business cycles are commonly estimated by the output gap, which is the difference between the actual and potential level of a national output, such as the country's GDP. Output gaps for different business cycles and fluctuations in GDP can subsequently be analysed to establish the level at which cycles move together. Traditionally, the correlation measure is used to assess cycle synchronicity; however, several criticisms are raised against this measure (Mink et al., 2007). Alternatively, Mink et al. (2007) use a non-parametric measure, which has several advantages over other measures, including the ease of interpretation and the ability to provide the direction of cycle synchronisation (Basher, 2010). The measure determines the synchronicity between a reference cycle—in this context the cycle of the oil sector—and another individual cycle, such as the cycle of the non-oil or manufacturing sector. Synchronisation could be between one single reference cycle and a group of cycles.

Methods used to estimate potential output (trend) and output gaps in this study, together with the Mink et al. (2007) synchronicity measure, are discussed as follows:

Estimating the output gap

The output gap is an unobservable variable defined as the difference between an actual and potential output. It is a commonly used instrument in policy formulation, playing a prominent role in macro-economic theory and in the practical development of monetary policy in many economies. Given other observable macro-economic variables, several techniques have been developed to estimate the potential output and the output gap. Three classes of techniques exist, all of which vary in regard to their usage of economic theory, namely statistical, structural and mixed or multivariate methods.

The estimation of potential output in this study is developed using a purely statistical approach, utilising the popular Hodrick-Prescott (HP) filter. This technique is known for its simplicity and has a multitude of advantages over several other techniques available in the literature (Cogley and Nason, 1995; Clark, 1989; Harvey and Jaeger, 1993; Ravn and Uhlig, 2002). No attempt is made to carry out an estimation using the structural or mixed approaches because the reliance of these approaches on economic theory and model assumptions make them more appropriate for industrialised economies (Osman et al., 2010).

The Hodrick-Prescott (HP)

The HP is a commonly used de-trending technique to estimate potential output, y_t^p and the related output gap. The HP filter computes the smoothed long-term component of output, y_t^p, by minimising the variance of output y_t around potential output y_t^p subject to a penalty that constrains the second difference of the potential output. Thus, the filter chooses the potential output, y_t^p, which minimises the quantity:

$$\sum_1^T \left(y_t - y_t^p\right)^2 + \sum_2^{T-1}\left(\left(y_{t+1}^p - y_t^p\right) - \left(y_t^p - y_{t-1}^p\right)\right)^2 \tag{1}$$

T indicates the sample size. The penalty parameter λ controls the smoothness of the trend output, y_t^p by capturing the importance of cyclical shocks to the output relative to trend output shocks. The penalty parameter is chosen arbitrarily. For annual data, Hodrick and Prescott selected a value of λ equals 100. Notably, the larger the value of λ, the smoother the trend becomes. Ravn and Uhlig (2002) suggested a proper value of λ equalling 6.25 for annual data.

The synchronisation measure

Let $g_r(t)$ denote the output gap associated with the reference cycle, the oil sector cycle. Mink et al.'s (2007) synchronicity measure between individual sector i (e.g. the manufacturing sector) and the reference cycle in period t is given as:

$$\varphi_{ir}(t) = \frac{g_i(t)g_r(t)}{\left(g_i(t)g_r(t)\right)} \tag{2}$$

$g_i(t)$ is the output gap for sector (e.g. the manufacturing sector) in period t.

The multivariate representation of Mink et al.'s synchronicity measure that examines synchronicity between a group of business cycles and a reference cycle is given as:

$$\varphi(t) = \frac{1}{N}\sum_1^N \frac{g_i(t)g_r(t)}{\left(g_i(t)g_r(t)\right)} \tag{3}$$

N is the number of business cycles in the group for the non-oil sectors within the country.

The synchronicity measure takes a value between −1 and +1. The measure will take the value 1 if both $g_i(t)$ and $g_r(t)$ have the same sign, and it takes the value −1 if their signs are opposites. Sector i is said to be dependent (synchronised) on the reference sector when the synchronicity measure approaches +1. The measure approaches −1 when output gaps do not coincide, and sector i is said to be independent of the reference sector: that happens when diversification occurs. The percentage of times sector i's output gaps have the same sign as the reference cycle in period t can be estimated by transforming the synchronicity measure to a uniform [0, 1] scale.

SECOND: UAE SUCCESS IN UTILISING KNOWLEDGE AND TECHNOLOGICAL INFRASTRUCTURE

In addition to the annual UAE GDP data 1975–2010, annual data from the UAE Bureau of Statistics on the country's foreign trade are also used to meet the second research objective, stated in the introduction of this chapter. The data cover technology products exports and imports for the 1981–2010 period. In this context, technology products are defined according to Revision 3 of the Standard International Trade Classification (SITC) retrieved from the World Trade Organization Statistical Database (2011). To realise the second objective, other international data sources are also used, including UNICAD, Scopus and the International Telecommunication Union databases.

To evaluate the extent of success the UAE achieved in utilising knowledge and available technological infrastructure to move towards a KE, the second objective, the time trend of exports and imports of UAE manufacturing and technology products were investigated. Countries that experience innovative sophisticated production processes are expected to enjoy a positive trade balance for technological products: higher exports than imports. Further, based on Porter's national competitiveness model, a regression analysis is employed to investigate factors that influence technology exports (excluding re-exports) originating in the UAE.

THIRD: UAE TRANSITION TO A KE, GLOBAL COMPETITIVENESS AND THE ROLE OF STI

The UAE global competitiveness and related analysis and discussions drew on the most recently available international data, including the World Bank Knowledge for Development (K4D) data sources, and data and measures made available from the World Economic Forum (WEF) 2011–2013 Global Competitiveness Report (GCR). Figure 4.1 illustrates the various components (categories, pillars and factors) of the GCI framework.

To explore the role of STI in transforming the UAE into a KE; initially, the country's achievements in implementing the KE pillars are assessed. Further, the country's STI capacity and competence in exercising the adoption and diffusion of knowledge are evaluated. A situational analysis and a comparative approach are utilised to realise this objective. In particular, the exercise evaluates the UAE experience within its GCC regional domain, together with that of few examples from transformation economies such as Singapore and the Republic of Korea.

World Bank Knowledge Assessment Methodology (KAM)

The World Bank KAM (www.worldbank.org/kam) was utilised to provide an overview of the UAE's and the other selected countries worldwide performance based on the four pillars of the KE. Eventually, the KAM KEI and the KAM KI are deployed to gauge the conduciveness of

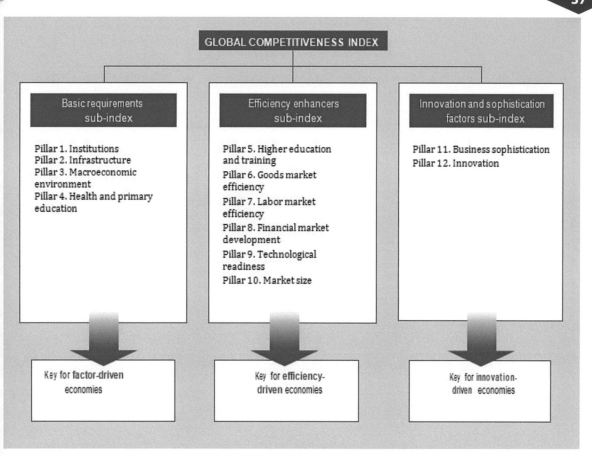

Source: World Economic Forum.

Figure 4.1

The global competitiveness index framework

the country's environment for an effective use of knowledge in the economic development process, and to assess the country's competence in exercising the adoption and diffusion of knowledge.

The KEI and KI indices, and several other KAM descriptive tools, generally rely on a set of normalised indicators (with values ranging from a minimum of 0 to a maximum of 10) that are measured for a reference year, 1995, and for the most recent period, governed by the availability of data. It is important to note that the KEI represents a simple average of the normalised values of the 12 knowledge indicators shown in Figure 4.2. The KI is also a simple average of indicators representing three key KE pillars indicated in Figure 4.1. Some of the KAM indicators are usually weighted by the country's population size in order to control for the effect of strong economies.

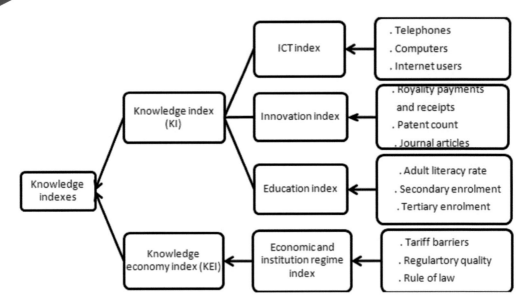

Source: World Bank Knowledge for Development (K4D).

Figure 4.2

Variables (indicators) forming the KEI and the KI indexes

CONCLUSIONS

In the next chapter, results based on the HP statistical technique will be used to estimate the output gap for the oil and manufacturing sectors in order to investigate the UAE's diversification towards manufacturing sectors. Also, summary statistics and regression analysis results will be used to discuss the level of the UAE's success in developing indigenous technological capabilities and innovating manufacturing and production processes.

5
CHAPTER

ECONOMIC DIVERSIFICATION AND KNOWLEDGE UTILISATION

INTRODUCTION

The focus of this chapter is to empirically evaluate the extent of the UAE's success in diversifying its economy and utilising knowledge and available technological infrastructure in domesticating the manufacture and production of technology products as important sources of wealth generation. The chapter will therefore provide a strong case for diversifying the UAE economy and implementing the principles and approaches of KE in the country.

THE UAE OIL AND MANUFACTURING SECTOR OUTPUT GAP

Figure 5.1 displays UAE real oil and non-oil sectors GDPs for the 1975–2010 period. The figure provides evidence of a slow increase in the growth rate of the UAE's oil GDP, subsequent to the removal of the 1973 oil embargo. This is followed by a declining trend that is clearly evident during the mid-1980s in response to a collapse in oil prices. The rates after the 1990 Gulf War illustrate a constant growth. The trend of non-oil GDP, on the other hand, demonstrates a gradual rise in growth rates until approximately 1990, followed by a steady increase afterwards, which appears to reflect the success of the UAE's diversification strategy of promoting non-hydrocarbon sectors. A similar post-1990 increase is noticed (Figure 5.1) in the manufacturing sector trend, albeit at a very slow pace.

As is clearly depicted in Figure 5.2, the HP filter indicates that the UAE oil output gap has sharply turned negative on two occasions: the mid- to late-1970s and the mid-1980s. Both occasions are associated with drops in oil prices. A close look at Figure 5.2 suggests that positive and negative output gaps for the oil and manufacturing sectors are somehow synchronised: positive (negative) growth in oil and manufacturing output gaps are generally related. This association is also confirmed by KAMCO (2011) on the premise that the expected increase in oil and gas prices would help derive GDP growth in the short-term. In addition, it would help the UAE government's expansionary fiscal policies to ensure the expansion of non-oil sectors, and the redirection of hydrocarbon revenues towards both the development of key industries and the funding of the costly processes for building domestic technology (Muysken and Nour, 2006). Basher (2010) argues that changes in oil prices may not have

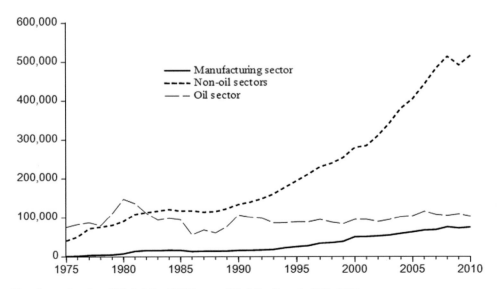

Source: Oil and non-oil sectors GDP statistics, UAE Bureau of Statistics Reports, 1975–2010.

Figure 5.1

UAE oil, manufacturing and non-oil sectors GDP (AED millions, 2001 = 100), 1975–2010

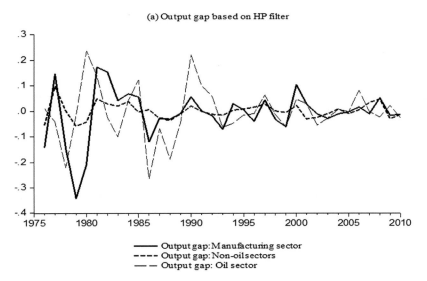

(a) Output gap based on HP filter

— Output gap: Manufacturing sector
---- Output gap: Non-oil sectors
— — Output gap: Oil sector

Source: Oil, non-oil and manufacturing sectors GDP statistics, UAE Bureau of Statistics reports, 1975–2010.

Figure 5.2

Oil sector, manufacturing sector and total non-oil sectors output gap based on the HP filter

any independent impact on the non-oil sector unless revenues are channelled through the government's fiscal instruments. This argument supports earlier evidence based on the empirical panel regression results produced by Husain et al. (2008), using data for ten oil-producing countries. The regression results suggest that oil prices do not independently influence underlying non-oil output.

KNOWLEDGE UTILISATION

A strategic goal of the UAE's diversification strategy is the expansion of the non-oil sectors to enhance the country's economy and enable it to compete with emerging markets. The UAE vision 2021 and the federal strategy 2011–2013 advocate the increase of investment in science and technology and R&D with the aim of turning the economy into a KE. This requires the adoption of strategies aimed at building local capacity, reducing dependence on foreign technologies, improving competitiveness and intensifying domestic manufacture and the production of technology products and equipment to serve both domestic and international needs. Recent statistics reveal that the UAE manufacturing productivity and its contribution to the GDP has increased slowly over time, as shown in Figure 5.1. However, the extent at which the current diversification levels towards the manufacturing sector are minimising reliance on the oil sector needs further investigation.

A review of Figure 5.3, which displays the synchronicity of the manufacturing sector with the oil sector (together with the calculated trend), estimated using the Hodrick-Prescott (HP) filter (see methodology in Chapter 4), reveals the following insights. There are some occasions where the manufacturing sector trend showed an increased dependence on the oil sector, in particular during the 1980s and the late 1990s.

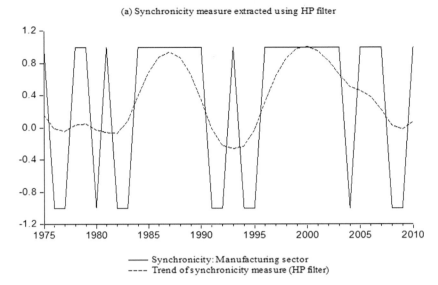

(a) Synchronicity measure extracted using HP filter

——— Synchronicity: Manufacturing sector
---- Trend of synchronicity measure (HP filter)

Source: Oil and manufacturing sectors GDP Statistics, UAE Bureau of Statistics Reports, 1975–2010.

Figure 5.3

The synchronicity of the UAE manufacturing sector and the UAE oil sector based on the HP filter

An overall assessment of the level of dependence and independence of the manufacturing sector on the oil sector from 1975–2010 can be further estimated by looking at the percentage of times the manufacturing and oil sectors had output gaps with the same sign. Using the HP filter, the reported percentage of output gaps with the same sign for the two sectors reached 66.7%, which signifies a high level of manufacturing sector dependence on the oil sector. However, the post-2000 synchronicity trend, shown in Figure 5.3, indicated a significant erosion of the dependence level, suggesting that the diversification of the UAE economy within the manufacturing sector started to show higher levels of development and signs of increased independence from the oil sector.

Indeed, reviewing the summary given in Table 5.1, there is a clear indication that the manufacturing sector is gaining momentum and that its contribution to both the total GDP and the non-oil GDP is increasing over time. However, one important characteristic of the UAE manufacturing sector is its labour-intensive nature, which is strained by relatively low labour productivity. This is caused by the adoption of production processes that mainly rely on unskilled and relatively inexpensive foreign labour (Abdalla et al., 2008). In addition to fostering a culture that values scientific and technological innovation, building a KE requires more investment in the acquisition of advanced technologies and the development of high levels of competency in the workforce (World Bank, 2005b).

According to Seyoum (2004), a good measure of a country's competitiveness in high technology is the presence of substantial and sustained exports in the high technology sector. By increasing the overall efficiency of labour and capital, high technology sectors contribute

Year	Contribution of manufacturing GDP as a percentage of non-oil GDP	Contribution of manufacturing GDP as a percentage of total GDP
[1970, 1980]	03.79	01.64
[1980, 1990]	11.83	06.62
[1990, 2000]	12.72	08.53
[2000, 2010]	15.64	12.39
All	12.12	08.22

Table 5.1   The contribution of manufacturing GDP as a percentage of non-oil GDP and total GDP

Source: Non-oil and manufacturing sectors GDP Statistics, UAE Bureau of Statistics Reports, 1970–2010.

to rapid growth in both manufacturing and services (Seyoum, 2005). He further echoed a statement by Reich (1991) that high-technology industries will replace resource and labour capital-intensive industries as the future primary source of wealth generation.

The aforementioned discussion stimulates a need to further investigate the UAE's success in developing indigenous technological capabilities, and innovating manufacturing and production processes. The discussion will also further investigate the level of technology transfer made thus far in achieving the country's transition into a KE. Such investigation would utilise a number of indicators, including the country's exports and imports of technological products. Technological products are often linked to firms and industries whose products or services embody advanced and innovative technologies (Keeble and Wilkinson, 2000). These firms commonly rely on advanced scientific and technological expertise and high R&D expenditure.

The UAE technology imports and exports data depicted in Figure 5.4 and Table 5.2 indicate an increasingly chronic balance of payments deficit in technology as a result of increased dependence on technology imports. This dependence is due to the country's lag in many important areas, such as investment in domestic knowledge innovations and the promotion of growth in a skilled workforce (Abdalla et al., 2008). Nevertheless, as Seyoum (2005) argues, "For many countries, high technology development may not be easily realised just through domestic innovative activity".

The experience of many successful economies shows that besides internal technology development, external sources of technology can be identified and acquired through licensing of foreign technology, Foreign Direct Investment (FDI) and acquisition of foreign high technology companies or even importation of high technology products. Even though governments tend to focus on the production of technology, it is the consumption of it that has the greater impact. An OECD study (1997) on the role of R&D spending and foreign technology acquisition spending reported greater productivity gains and higher investment returns from buying rather than producing new technology.

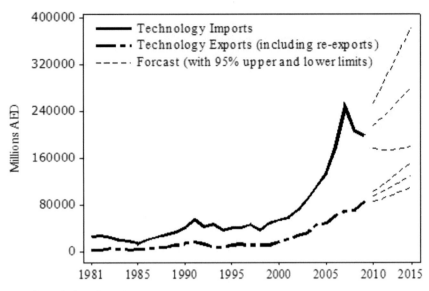

Source: Abdalla, Alfaki and Ahmed (2013).

Figure 5.4

UAE technology products imports and exports (millions AED) together with (2011–2015) forecast based on ARIMA (0, 2, 1) model

	Table 5.2	UAE technology products deficit (exports—imports in millions AED)	
Year	*Mean*	*Median*	*Standard deviation*
[1981, 1985]	18,557	18,295	4384
[1986, 1990]	16,753	17,264	5249
[1991, 1995]	33,261	31,276	5244
[1996, 2000]	32,179	30,767	5065
[2001, 2005]	48,690	43,736	12,989
[2006, 2010]	125,987	116,919	34,658
[2011, 2015]	134,753	134,469	11,965

Source: Abdalla, Alfaki and Ahmed (2013).

Despite the high deficit in UAE technology exports (Figure 5.4 and Table 5.2), the country is riding an increasing trend of higher technology export growth, particularly since the year 2000. Studying 55 developed and developing countries, Seyoum (2005) discussed three factors hypothesised to influence a nation's level of high technology exports:

1   The level of FDI;
2   Domestic demand conditions and the sophistication of buyers;
3   The availability of the technological infrastructure.

These were recognised as external factors, as opposed to internal firm production factors, such as technology management and strategy.

Drawing on Seyoum's (2005) methodology, the rest of this chapter proposes an empirical investigation of factors that influence technology exports in the UAE. The investigation serves two purposes. First, it will assess the contribution of the UAE national technological infrastructure in enhancing the technology exports sector through increasing the efficiency of labour and capital. Second, it will investigate the country's orientation towards technological development through increasing R&D spending and upgrading necessary scientific and technological resources.

Therefore, a regression analysis is employed to investigate the relationship between UAE technology exports (excluding re-exports) and the factors highlighted by Seyoum's study (2005), based on Porter's model of national competitiveness (Porter, 1990). The utilised dataset represents a time series covering 2000–2010, obtained from the UAE Bureau of Statistics and other international sources.

A technological infrastructure constitutes the development of scientific and technological resources to support a nation's technology-based development. It is argued that competitiveness and trade performance in high-technology industries are strongly related to the level of R&D and the availability of highly skilled labour, scientists and engineers, important to create and sustain a significant level of innovative activity (Keeble and Wilkinson, 2000). To measure technological infrastructure, Seyoum (2005) used two variables: the country's expenditure on R&D and the number of scientists and engineers engaged in R&D.

To measure UAE technological infrastructure, four variables were used. The first variable represents *the proportion of skilled workers* (i.e. those with an education above high-school level), obtained from the UAE census and the Ministry of Labour estimates (Al Awad, 2010). The second variable denotes *the number of publications by UAE scientists and researchers in the science fields* retrieved from the Scopus database (SCImago, 2007). The third and fourth variables are *the number of UAE Internet and broadband subscriptions per 100 inhabitants*, retrieved from the International Telecommunication Union database (http://www.itu.int/ITU-D/ict/statistics/). Each variable is standardised to the same scale to have a mean of zero and a standard deviation of one. Subsequently, an index denoted as the UAE *Technological Infrastructure Index (TII)* was formed as a simple average of the four standardised variables. This index is believed to capture the state of the scientific infrastructure in the UAE.

On the other hand, FDI, retrieved from the UNICAD database, is believed to generate several positive effects on host economies. These range from the transfer of advanced and new technologies to the host economy, to the establishment of collaboration and alliances between foreign and local firms in the host economy (Seyoum, 2005). Collaboration arrangements often take the form of long-term supply arrangements between firms, joint R&D, joint ventures and licenses, all of which lead to the development and exportation of new and advanced products.

The dependent variable in the regression model, *UAE technology exports in Billion UAE Dirhams*, is log transformed to normalise the distribution. The independent variables are thus represented by the *inward FDI* and the developed *TII*. The third factor in Porters model, *home*

Table 5.3 Regression analysis results and parameter estimates				
Coefficient	Estimate	Standard error	t	P
Constant	0.655	0.1440	4.561	0.002
FDI	1.833×10^{-5}	0.0001	1.076	0.313
TII	0.816	0.0990	8.214	0.000
Adjusted R^2	0.921			
F value	46.383	(p-value = 0.00)		

demand conditions, is not included in the regression model due to the unavailability of data. It is worth noting that the World Economic Forum has published the *Buyers' Sophistication Index* as a proxy for home demand conditions at the country level in their Global Competitiveness Report (GCR) of 2004. The index was based on surveying experts and business leaders. However, during the period from 2004–2012, the GCR used different methodologies to estimate the index, and, therefore, resulting indices are not comparable over time.

Due to the time-series nature of the data used in the regression analysis, there is a large probability that model residuals may be time dependent, which may result in biasing the regression coefficients. However, diagnostics checks and the correlation of regression residuals and lagged residuals revealed a non-significant coefficient, $\rho = -0.106$, $p = 0.771$, leading to the conclusion that model's errors are independent. The fitted model demonstrates a high explanatory power with an adjusted coefficient of determination, R^2, reaching 92.1% of the total variations of the UAE technology exports.

Table 5.3 presents the results of the regression analysis. Evidence confirms the strong positive and highly significant relationship between technological infrastructure and technology exports ($p < -0.01$). Although the relationship between inward FDI and UAE technology exports is taking the expected positive direction (Table 5.3), it is clear that the role of inward FDI in promoting UAE technology exports is still insignificant ($p = 0.313$). Therefore, based on the regression analysis results, it could be argued that recent growth in UAE technology exports can be attributed mainly to increasing developments in the country's technological infrastructure. These developments themselves could be the result of recent increases in the supply of skilled labour and from increased levels of investment in R&D that might have led to increased research output. They could also, arguably, be related to developments in the ICT sector, indicated by the increased level of Internet and broadband subscriptions witnessed recently in the country.

CONCLUSIONS

This chapter has discussed the level of achievement that the UAE has attained; in diversifying its economy by expanding a profitable manufacturing sector, by promoting the application of knowledge and technology in efficient production and in the development of new domestic products. In the next chapter, we will explore the role of STI in transforming the UAE into a KE. We will also evaluate the country's STI capacity and competence in exercising adoption and diffusion of knowledge.

6

CHAPTER

SCIENCE, TECHNOLOGY AND INNOVATION IN UAE

INTRODUCTION

UAE Vision 2021 advocates increasing investment in Science, Technology and Innovation (STI) and Research and Development (R&D). Moreover, building a modern KE requires more investment in acquiring advanced technologies and high levels of competency in the workforce (see Aubert and Reiffers, 2003).

This chapter aims to explore the role of STI in transforming UAE into a KE by initially assessing the country's achievements in implementing the KE pillars. It further evaluates the country's STI capacity and competence in exercising adoption and diffusion of knowledge.

EDUCATION SYSTEM AND SKILLS

Today's globalising economy requires countries to nurture pools of well-educated workers who are able to adapt rapidly to their changing environment and the evolving needs of the production system (GCR, 2006–2013). The Executive opinion survey of the WEF of 2011–2012 revealed that, from a list of 15 factors, an inadequately educated workforce represented the third top problematic factor for doing business in the UAE. The quantity and quality of education, however (particularly basic education), are important prerequisites for increasing productivity and work efficiency. A workforce with little formal education is inclined to produce limited simple manual products. It also lacks the right skills and capabilities to absorb new technologies and generate new ideas and innovations that promote productivity and bring about new products.

Recent growth in the UAE's economy was marked by an increase in the low-skilled and low-paid labour force (Abdalla et al., 2010). According to the last UAE census in 2005, foreign workers represented more than 92% of the employed workforce: around 11% were illiterate, 16% were able to read and write and around 53% had an education level between primary and secondary. Slightly more than 20% had an education level above secondary school (e.g. diploma, university degree, Master's degree or PhD). Assuming that workers with secondary education or above are skilled, Al Awad (2010) indicated that the percentage of unskilled workers in the UAE represented 80% of the employed labour force. If left to market forces, profit maximising employers in the private sector will prefer to continue to hire foreign workers at significantly lower wage rates. However, building a modern KE requires more investment in acquiring advanced technologies and high levels of competency in the workforce. Today's globalising economy requires countries to nurture pools of well-educated workers who are able to adapt rapidly to their changing environment and the evolving needs of the production system (GCR, 2011–2012). The UAE is, therefore, in great need of putting in place a mix of policies and plans that can help raise the skill level of the country's labour force.

The percentage of adult literacy in the UAE among the population aged 15 years or above is 90.5%, similar to that of Qatar and second after Kuwait, when compared within the GCC countries domain. In this context, Singapore and the Republic of Korea have reached 94.4 and 97.9% in literacy rates, respectively. The gross in secondary education enrolment rate reached 92.4%, better only than the percentages of Oman and Kuwait of 89.8 and 88.7, respectively. These can be compared to Singapore's and the Republic of Korea's rates of 63.2 and 97.5%, respectively. In tertiary education, the UAE scored a gross rate of 22.9; fourth place of GCC countries after Bahrain (32.1), Oman (25.5) and Saudi Arabia (30.2). In this domain, Singapore and the Republic of Korea achieved higher growth rates of 55.9 and 94.7, respectively.

Education figures based on UNESCO data sources reflect the poor performance of UAE in terms of expenditure on education. In 2006, the country devoted only 1.1% of its GDP to education, the lowest compared to the Republic of Korea (4.2%) and all other GCC countries: Saudi Arabia (6.2%), Oman (3.9%), Kuwait (3.8%) and Bahrain (3.4%). Similar spending patterns persisted throughout 2007 (1.0%) and 2009 (1.2%). Nevertheless, according to the GCR of 2011–2012, the UAE has made significant progress in secondary (95.2%) and tertiary (30.4%)

education enrolment compared to 2009 KAM figures. This is on a par with Saudi Arabia (96.8%) and Bahrain (96.4%) at the secondary level, better than the performance of the rest of the GCC countries, but still below that of Singapore and the Republic of Korea in both levels. In Singapore, for instance, education is highly subsidised by the government—constituting the second-largest expenditure item—providing the country with the higher technical skills and training needed for high-technology production (Radwan and Pellegrini, 2010).

It is instructive to note that the higher education sector in the UAE has witnessed a large expansion, with the number of licensed colleges and universities increasing from 5 in 1997 to about 58 in 2008, including some foreign universities who established branch campuses (Hijazi et al., 2008). Only three of these institutions are government funded institutions; namely, the UAE University, Zayed University and the High Colleges of Technology (HCT). The expansion in higher education opportunities was mainly driven by the high economic growth in the UAE economy and the increase in investments made by the private sector in higher education institutions in the Gulf region in general (Lefrere, 2007).

To improve the quality of education at the public universities, the UAE Government devised various initiatives, including seeking accreditation of both institutions and individual academic programmes from mainly North American higher education accreditation agencies. Similar national agencies were established to oversee the quality of education within the private institutions; these included the UAE Commission for the Academic Accreditation (CAA) and the Knowledge and Human Development Authority in Dubai. Despite these progressive improvements in the size and the quality of higher education, there still remains a significant mismatch between UAE labour market needs and the kind of specialisations obtained by graduates of UAE higher education institutions (Hijazi et al., 2008). From the 2005 figures, it can been seen that about one-third of higher education graduates studied an STI curriculum and the other two-thirds were graduates of social sciences tracks. This result does not support labour market needs and future plans to increase growth in the innovation system, which is very much in need of the development of human resources in engineering, science and technology.

Reviewing the quality of the education system, the 2011–2012 GCR positioned the UAE 29th; far below the rankings of Singapore (2nd), Qatar (4th) and Saudi Arabia (25th), but better than the Republic of Korea (55th) and the rest of the GCC countries: Kuwait (108th), Oman (46th) and Bahrain (31st). Indeed, the current worldwide position of the UAE education system (29th) has prompted the 2011–2012 GCR to suggest prioritising further investment to boost educational outcomes, arguing that raising the bar with respect to education will require not only measures to improve the quality of teaching and the relevance of the curriculum, but also incentivising the population to attend schools at primary and secondary levels as well.

INNOVATION

Transition to a KE is greatly dependent on the development of innovation capacities that are strongly interlinked with the level of education, qualifications and skills building in the community (see Ahmed and Al-Roubaie, 2012; Zahlan, 2007).

Table 6.1	Arab countries innovation index, 2014	
Rank	Country	Score
36	United Arab Emirates	43.2
38	Saudi Arabia	41.6
47	Qatar	40.3
54	Turkey	38.2
62	Bahrain	36.3
64	Jordan	36.2
65	Armenia	36.1
69	Kuwait	35.2
74	Georgia	34.5
75	Oman	33.9
77	Lebanon	33.6
78	Tunisia	32.9
84	Morocco	32.2
99	Egypt	30.0
101	Azerbaijan	29.6
133	Algeria	24.2
141	Yemen	19.5

Source: Cornell University, INSEAD, and WIPO (2014).

Based on the recent GII 2014 published by Cornell University, INSEAD and WIPO (2014), Table 6.1 provides an overview of some selected Arab countries showing high performance in terms of innovation outputs surmounting weaknesses from the input side, and those that lag behind in fulfilling their innovation potential. From the analysis in Table 6.1, UAE scores 43.2 and is ranked 36th in the world, leading the Arab countries.

The principal challenges facing UAE and most Arab countries revolve around an inability to create knowledge and generate innovation to support the KE. Building capacity for STI in UAE by strengthening knowledge production, sharing, distribution and transfer, technological learning and skill development is an essential condition to create a knowledge-based economy. In this endeavour, collaboration on the part of the public and private sectors is essential to generate linkages within various sectors of the economy. Moreover, GII 2011 highlights the needs for Arab countries to formulate carefully crafted policies that focus on creating linkages between the local and global knowledge systems, without succumbing to the pitfall of falling into undue dependency on global knowledge. Such dependency risks sacrificing long-term interest in favour of short- and medium-term, in as much as it entails forfeiting the building of capacity to generate indigenous knowledge. Without indigenous knowledge, development will be constrained, if not hobbled, by foreign knowledge in the long term.

R&D ACTIVITIES

Most private companies in the Middle East and North Africa (MENA) and the GCC region lack the incentives, capacity and skills to innovate (UNDP, 2002, 2003). Only 3% of the R&D in the Arab countries is funded by the private sector, compared to more than 5% in OECD countries.

The UAE ranked 32 out of 142 countries in terms of the capacity of its companies and people to create, and then commercialise, new products and processes (GCR, 2011–2012). This positioned UAE in third place within the GCC context, after Qatar (11th out of 142) and Saudi Arabia (21st), and below Singapore (22nd) and the Republic of Korea (20th). Among the basic foundations of a country's innovation infrastructure is its R&D activities and the pool of scientists and researchers able to play a part and contribute to innovation and the creation of new technologies (Chen and Dahlman, 2006).

Outcomes of the R&D activities can be realised and measured, utilising a number of indicators, including government and private sector spending on the education system and research, and collaboration between the industry and research institutions. Although the GCC countries have maintained developed world levels of GDP per capita, investment in R&D still remains at developing world levels (McGlennon, 2006).

The UAE's performance on "company spending on R&D" and "University-industry collaboration in R&D" ranked 24th and 37th worldwide, respectively, trailing most industrialised and transformation economy countries, including Singapore (10th and 6th) and the Republic of Korea (11th and 25th). Within the GCC region, the country's performance is average, occupying third place after Qatar (20th and 10th) and Saudi Arabia (18th and 28th). Disclosure of information about the level of financial resources devoted to R&D in the UAE is scarce; most available information is based on estimations made by international sources.

A collective review of spending on R&D activities in the GCC countries, of which the UAE is no exception, reveals the public sector as the main contributor, accounting for 49.4% of the total R&D spending by all sectors and institutions (Nour, 2005). Universities in the region also provide a sizable contribution of about 43.5%, leaving the private sector with a minute share of 7.1%. Given the strong link between R&D and innovative activities required to sustain growth and development, the private sector in the GCC countries is thus playing an insignificant role in the process of transfer to KE. It largely tends to utilise research done by international companies (UNDP, 2009). Within the Republic of Korea, the private sector has succeeded in increasing the country's indigenous innovation, and promoting inward transfer of foreign technologies and development of domestic innovation and production capacity, by mainly relying on R&D (World Bank, 2006).

According to UNESCO, Korean investment on R&D activities, as a share of the country's GDP, increased from 2.48% in 2004 to 3.36% in 2008, with the private sector accounting for about three-quarters of this share. Similar patterns of investment increase in R&D can be noted in the Singaporean model, with the share of GDP increasing from 2.13% in 2004 to 2.66% in 2008. It is informative to note that the Singaporean Government plays a very active role in innovation by stimulating private sector R&D through allocating significant funds to support public sector R&D, and by setting strategic directions intended to promote specific industries (Radwan and Pellegrini, 2010).

In 2008, the UAE government established the "National Research Foundation (NRF)" with a vision of bringing together all universities and research institutions in the country to support world-class research activities and create an internationally competitive research environment and innovation system. It is envisaged that the expected outcomes of these research activities will bridge the gap between the UAE and the industrialised countries in technology absorption and creation, enhancing productivity and enabling the businesses of the UAE to be more competitive. Over the ensuing years, employing international standards, the foundation received and vigorously reviewed a significant number of grant proposals in science, technology and social science disciplines, on the basis of the National Priorities Research programme. These covered almost all universities and colleges in the country. However, it was unfortunate that the launch of the NRF programme coincided with the 2008 world economic crisis, resulting in major funding cuts and delays in the grant-awarding process. The contributions of the NRF towards fulfilling its mission and bringing the scientific and research community closer to the business and labour market needs are yet to be clearly realised. The country could benefit immensely from the experience of several successful transformation economies, enabling it to adapt similar models that can also yield to domestic boundaries and constraints.

KNOWLEDGE PRODUCTION: SIZE AND QUALITY OF RESEARCH PUBLICATIONS

Useful and frequently used indicators for gauging a country's scientific activities are to assess the availability of scientists and engineers in the country and the number of research publications in refereed international journals per population. According to the GCR of 2011–2012, the UAE scored 4.95 points on availability of scientists and engineers. This score is based on a 1 to 7 scale; a value of 7 means that scientists and engineers are widely available, while a value of 1 means that they are non-existent. This good score positioned the country top of all GCC countries and the Republic of Korea (see Figure 6.1). The actual implication of this outcome is that the UAE has a high potential to advance research and innovations in both size and quality.

However, the country's performance in the international list of published research (1996–2010) stayed low, scoring 12,914 published papers in this period (Figure 6.2). This statistic positioned the country second after Saudi Arabia, GCC-wise, and 66th worldwide. The statistics can also be interpreted to imply the country's inability to utilise and incentivise the widely available pool of researchers in its arena. Despite the fact that Saudi Arabia and the Republic of Korea have smaller pools of scientists and engineers than the UAE (Figure 6.1), their share of internationally published research is almost three times and 33 times more than that of the UAE, respectively (Figure 6.2). This disparity could partially be attributed to the lack of sufficient funds and cooperation between scientists. The UAE is, therefore, in great need of initiating proactive measures and social conditions to enable a process of cooperation and

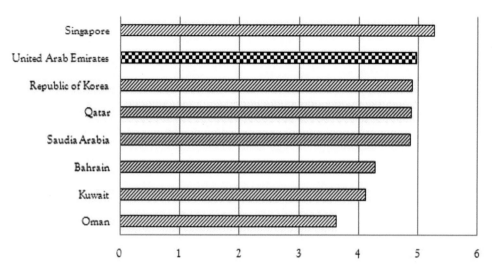

Source: Global Competitiveness Report (WEF), 2011–2012.

Figure 6.1

Availability of scientists and engineers

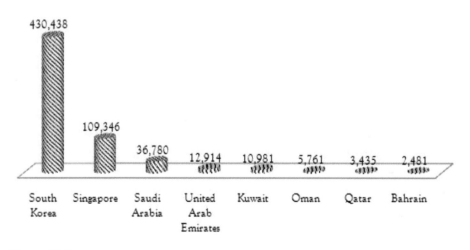

Source: SCImago (2007).

Figure 6.2

Research publications (1996–2010)

interaction between scientists and researchers domestically. Such a process of cooperation and interaction, particularly in science and technology, would lead an improvement in the conduct of scientific research and an increase in the number of co-authored publications. It would also ensure the quality and success of scientific enterprises (Zahlan, 2007).

Based on the Hirsch index (H-index), using the SCImago (2007) updated database for 2012, the quality and impact of research published by UAE scholars (1996–2010), received an

H-index value of 72, ranking the country 66th in a list of 236 countries worldwide. This position placed the UAE above all other GCC countries, except Saudi Arabia who scored 106 (ranking it 50th). Singapore's H-index was 218, placing the country 32nd, and the Republic of Korea scored 287, securing rank 14 in the list. Evaluating the quality of published work in terms of the number of citations per document, the UAE, in parity with Kuwait, occupied the top of the list, GCC-wise, with scores of 7.02 and 7.06 citations per document, respectively. This is below both Singapore and the Republic of Korea's scores of 11.82 and 9.82, respectively. Evidence indicates an increasing trend in the level of the UAE's internationally collaborative research (see Figure 6.3), as more than 58% of research documents published by UAE scholars during 1996–2010 were co-authored with researchers from foreign institutions (SCImago, 2007). A similar trend, albeit on a lower scale, can be observed for Saudi Arabia (see Figure 6.3).

The tendency of the UAE and other Arab world scientists towards international collaboration, as suggested by UNDP (2009), is prompted by a lack of domestic funding and the fact that most industrialised countries encourage their scientists to collaborate internationally. Further explanations highlight the growing connectivity between scientists worldwide, and, more importantly, the tendency of UAE-employed professors—mainly expatriates—to retain ties and links with their own countries and institutes of origin (Bachellerie, 2010). Countries such as the Republic of Korea have managed to increase private sector investment in R&D, have succeeded in promoting inter-country research connectivity and have benefitted from international programmes and partnerships. A quarter of Korea's research production between 1996 and 2010 was a result of global cooperation (see Figure 6.3.)

In 2007, the Statistical, Economic and Social Research and Training Centre for the Islamic Countries (SESRTCIC), ranked the UAE University (UAEU), the biggest publicly funded institution in the country; ninth out of 84 universities in the Islamic countries and top of all

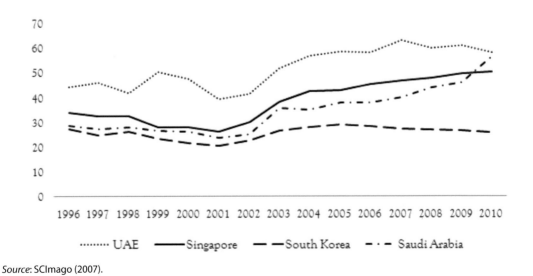

Source: SCImago (2007).

Figure 6.3

Percentage of country publications with international collaboration (1996–2010)

universities in the GCC countries. In research quality, measured as the number of citations per published paper, the UAEU scored an average of 0.53. Also, in research performance, measured by the number of published papers per number of faculty, the university scored 0.40. Both scores positioned the UAEU among the 20 top universities in the Islamic world.

PUBLICATIONS IN STI AND PATENTS GRANTS

Publications in STI are used as an indicator of the ability and competence of researchers in a country and as a measure of the country's future potential for innovations and technical developments. GCC-wise, UAE publications in this category are in third place after Saudi Arabia and Kuwait (see Figure 6.4). However, the country's performance in this category, compared to the two benchmark innovation-driven economies, Singapore and the Republic of Korea, is very low, representing respectively, about 6% and 1% of their publications in science and technology (Figure 6.4).

Bachellerie (2010) and Zahlan (2012) show that in the 1995–2009 period, science and engineering publications reached a total of 4925 papers, covering 16 UAE universities. This represented 93% of the total national science publications, stressing the dominance of universities in UAE scientific production. The majority of these published papers were in the field of medicine, followed by papers in engineering. The UAE University dominated the distribution of the production with over 60% of the total published science and engineering papers, followed by the American University of Sharja with 11%, Sharja University with 9%, the Petroleum Institute with 5%; the rest went to other universities in the country. More than 80% of these publications were a result of international cooperation, again reflecting

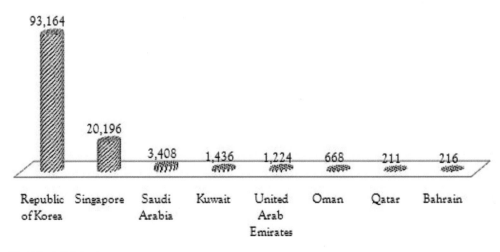

Source: World Bank Databank.

Figure 6.4

STI publications (2002–2007)

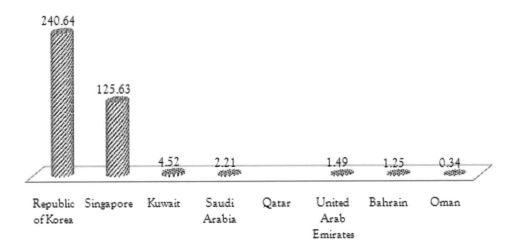

240.64

125.63

4.52   2.21   1.49   1.25   0.34

Republic   Singapore   Kuwait   Saudi   Qatar   United   Bahrain   Oman
of Korea   Arabia   Arab
                                               Emirates

Source: Global Competitiveness Report (WEF) (2011–2012).

Figure 6.5

Utility patents per million population

the low level of local cooperation among researchers in the UAE. Empowering the UAE NRF initiative with the needed resources and power to bring together all universities and research institutions in the country would help in developing and sustaining research capacity in areas that are of relevance to domestic needs. This would then encourage an exchange of ideas and information and create a scientific research system in which internal and external cooperation generates new knowledge and encourages patents and innovative thinking.

Granted utility patents are usually utilised as an indicator to provide a measure of the level of R&D and innovation capabilities in a country (World Bank, 2006). During the 1997–2010 period, the UAE filed 85 patents to the US Patents and Trademarks Office (USPTO), representing 1.49 per million population (Figure 6.5). This is an average performance when UAE is compared to regional GCC counterparts, but very weak compared to industrialised countries and the emerging transformation economies of Singapore (125.63 per million population) and the Republic of Korea (240.64 per million population).

CONCLUSIONS

The analysis and discussion conducted throughout this chapter drew on several international data sources that provided the basis for demonstrating the UAE's innovation capacity and readiness to compete in the global KE. The country's performance was evaluated worldwide and benchmarked against that of neighbouring GCC countries, together with other examples from the Asian transformation economies. In the next chapter, we will assess and evaluate the UAE's performance in terms of global competitiveness and technological readiness.

7
CHAPTER

TECHNOLOGICAL READINESS AND COMPETITIVENESS

WASD

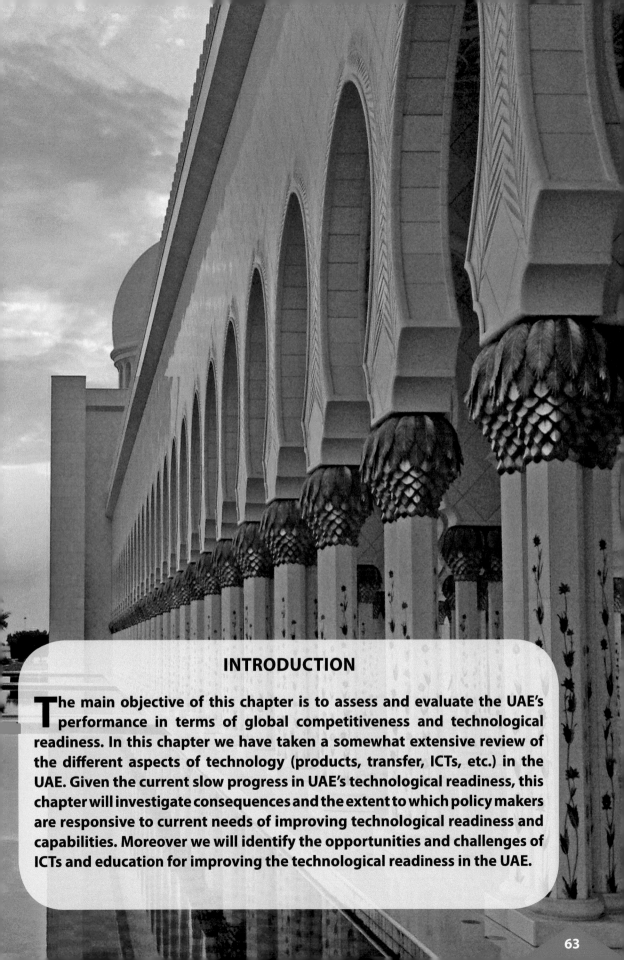

INTRODUCTION

The main objective of this chapter is to assess and evaluate the UAE's performance in terms of global competitiveness and technological readiness. In this chapter we have taken a somewhat extensive review of the different aspects of technology (products, transfer, ICTs, etc.) in the UAE. Given the current slow progress in UAE's technological readiness, this chapter will investigate consequences and the extent to which policy makers are responsive to current needs of improving technological readiness and capabilities. Moreover we will identify the opportunities and challenges of ICTs and education for improving the technological readiness in the UAE.

TECHNOLOGICAL READINESS

Table 7.1, adopted from the World Economic Forum's (WEF) various reports (GCR, 2006–2015), shows the percentage changes in UAE GCI performance worldwide. According to the analysis in Table 7.1, UAE performance has been the best within the MENA region for almost all the eight years investigated in this study, except in few parameters. In 2006, UAE is only lower than Algeria in the third pillar (macro-economic environment); also UAE is ranked 27th worldwide in 2011, slipping two positions from the 2010 ranking, below Qatar (14th) and Saudi Arabia (17th). However, according to the recent report from the WEF (2014), UAE is leading the Arab Region in the GCI, moving up to 12th position in 2014. It is also important to note the recent successful bid by UAE for Expo 2020, as well as many other national initiatives to enhance competitiveness.

However, elaborating on the UAE's loss of two places for the second year in a row, the recent GCR identified a number of areas of deterioration. The most noticeable was the country's loss of ability to use the latest technology for productivity improvements, which goes in line with the issue of unskilled labour in the country, highlighted in a previous chapter in this book. Table 7.2 provides more details about the various factors impacting UAE's technological readiness pillar as a percentage change between 2006 and 2012.

Table 7.1   Percentage change of UAE GCI (2006–2014)

	2006	2014	% Change
Overall GCI	37	12	25
A – Basic requirements	21	2	19
1st pillar: Institutions	24	7	17
2nd pillar: Infrastructure	17	3	14
3rd pillar: Macro-economic environment	7	5	2
4th pillar: Health and primary education	84	38	46
B – Efficiency enhancers	38	14	24
5th pillar: Higher education and training	57	6	51
6th pillar: Goods market efficiency	27	3	24
7th pillar: Labour market efficiency	22	8	14
8th pillar: Financial market development	48	17	31
9th pillar: Technological readiness	35	24	11
10th pillar: Market size	51	46	5
C – Innovation and sophistication factors	39	21	18
11th pillar: Business sophistication	31	14	17
12th pillar: Innovation	48	24	24

Source: Adopted from WEF (Global Competitiveness Reports, 2006–2015).

Table 7.2   Detailed analysis (percentage change) of UAE technological readiness (2006–2014)

	2006	2014	% Change
Technological readiness	35	24	11
Availability of latest technologies	14	8	6
Firm-level technology absorption	20	7	13
FDI and technology transfer	25	3	22
Individuals using Internet (% of pop.)	36	10	26
Broadband Internet subscriptions/100 pop.	43	61	–18
Int'l Internet bandwidth, kb/s per user	–	51	–
Mobile broadband subscriptions/100 pop.	–	11	–

Source: Adopted from WEF (Global Competitiveness Reports, 2006–2015).

Table 7.3   UAE technological readiness pillar (2006–2012)

	2012	2011	2010	2009	2008	2007	2006
Technological readiness	32	30	14	17	28	33	35
Availability of latest technologies	23	25	11	8	17	16	14
Firm-level technology absorption	12	16	5	4	14	17	20
FDI and technology transfer	6	10	6	6	15	13	25
Individuals using Internet, %	34	19	10	2	37	37	36
Broadband Internet subscriptions/100 pop.	52	49	39	40	43	45	43

Source: Adopted from WEF (Global Competitiveness Reports, 2006–2012).

The most noticeable decline was in the "technological readiness" pillar; from position 14 in 2010 to position 30 in 2011, then from position 32 in 2012 to its current position 24 (see Tables 7.2 and 7.3). This drop in the "technological readiness" pillar, however, could mean that others have developed technologically in a faster rhythm than the UAE.

However, in the context, Bachellerie (2010) debated the classification of the UAE by the WEF GC report as an "innovation-driven economy". He argued that the UAE has only satisfied the "factor-driven" stage of competitiveness, characterised by high performance in infrastructure and macro-economic environment. However, it does not show the strong performance that qualifies for membership of the second stage, "efficiency-driven economy". Within the GC context, the efficiency-driven stage is realised by a high performance in indicators such as availability of latest technologies, firm-level technology absorption and FDI and technology transfer, all of which reported low scores in the UAE compared to countries that have achieved the innovation-driven stage. According to the WEF GC report, the efficiency-driven stage entails maintenance of competitiveness through design and development of cutting-edge products and processes in an environment that is conducive to innovative activities. This should be supported by adequate public and private sector investments in R&D that bring together collaboration between research institutions and the industry.

TECHNOLOGY PRODUCTS

As stated earlier, one of the downsides affecting the UAE competitiveness (cited by the WFE GC report 2011–2012) was the country's inability to adapt and absorb exogenous technology for productivity improvements. Bachellerie (2010) reported an increasing domestic demand for technology products and equipment matched with insufficient domestic production, leading to high dependency on foreign technology imports and consequently impacting on the national balance of trade.

Table 7.4 displays the size of imports and exports of technology products, defined according to Revision 3 of the Standard International Trade Classification (SITC) retrieved from the World Trade Organization Statistical Database (2011) for the UAE, the rest of the GCC countries and other selected countries. These products mainly cover SITC Sections 5–8 minus division 68 and group 891; namely iron and steel, chemical products, machinery and transport equipment and others.

The UAE technology products' trade balance reported a trade deficit (exports minus imports) amounting to US\$43.01 billion in 2010; the second highest after Saudi Arabia (KSA) when compared to its GCC counterparts (Table 7.4). The UAE position reflects insufficient domestic technology production to cover domestic needs, contrasting the positions of Singapore and the Republic of Korea, who succeeded in sustaining a trade surplus in technology products (Table 7.4).

The UAE 2010 trade deficit in technology products represented about 14.2% of the country's GDP; third after Bahrain and Oman, eroding about 61% of the trade surplus in fuel and mining products. Despite this gloomy outcome, the UAE commands the highest percentage of exports in technology products (24%) compared to other GCC countries. Needless to say, the UAE exports figures include technology re-exports, implying that only a segment of these exports are domestically produced (Bachellerie, 2010).

Table 7.4   Technology products imports and exports in GCC and other selected countries, 2010

Country	Technology products export	Technology products import	Trade balance	Trade balance as % of fuel and mining products surplus	Technology products exports as a % of total exports	Technology products imports as a % of total imports	Deficit in technology products trade as a % of GDP
UAE	52.76	95.77	−43.01	60.6	24.0	59.9	14.2
Qatar	03.34	20.47	−17.13	33.2	05.4	88.1	13.5
Bahrain	01.41	6.17	−04.76	49.0	10.3	61.7	21.0
Kuwait	4.83	18.30	−13.47	22.0	07.2	81.5	10.2
KSA	29.17	77.54	−48.37	23.6	11.7	79.9	10.8
Oman	03.97	14.18	−10.21	41.4	10.8	71.4	17.6
Singapore	254.20	201.75	52.45	–	72.2	64.9	–
Korea	411.53	239.62	171.91	–	88.2	56.4	–

Source: International Monetary Fund.

TECHNOLOGY TRANSFER

The UAE's demand for, and dependency on, foreign technology generated a negative upward trend of technology transfer. As illustrated in Figure 7.1, the size of technology products' trade deficit seemed to grow exponentially ($R^2 = 0.90$) over the period 1980–2010. Although the deficit is still high, it is noteworthy that the big jump that took place during the 2008 crisis came to settle down to pre-2008 figures, as depicted in Figure 7.1.

Excluding fuel and mining trade surplus (US$71.0 billion) from the national trade balance (US$60.0 billion) for 2010, the country would have run into a deficit of US$11.0 billion. This shows the importance of trade in technology products in determining the country's balance of trade, and underscores the lack of innovative activities and the inability of the UAE economy to assimilate and create new knowledge and technologies to cater for domestic needs.

Establishing an innovation system of a network of institutions, rules and procedures that influences the way in which a country acquires, creates, disseminates and uses knowledge and technology, is essential for the sustainability of economic growth (Chen and Dahlman, 2006). Innovation is mainly realised through strong performance of the education system and efficient R&D activities, with support coming from both the public and private sectors, availability of venture capital and intellectual property protection.

In terms of "basic requirements" for global competitiveness—including macro-economic environment and availability of infrastructure, and based on the recent GCR (2006–2013)—the UAE ranked among the top five countries in the world, above the rest of the GCC countries. However, the country occupied 22nd position and above the rest of the GCC

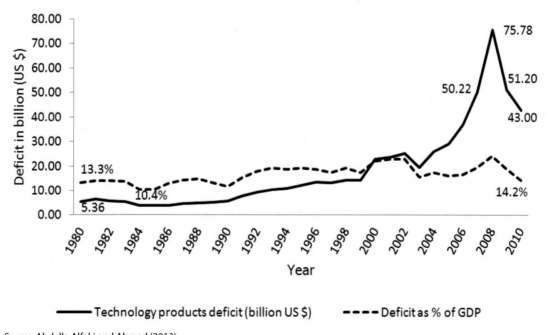

Technology products deficit (billion US $) ---- Deficit as % of GDP

Source: Abdalla Alfaki and Ahmed (2013).

Figure 7.1

UAE technology products deficit (in billions US$) and the percentage of deficits of the GDP

countries in the "efficiency enhancers" category, summarised by an index formed of several indicators including the country's technological readiness. Moreover, the UAE performance in government procurement of advanced technology products ranked 5th worldwide, after Qatar (1st), Singapore (2nd), Saudi Arabia (3rd) and Malaysia (4th) in 2011. All other GCC countries were within the top 20 countries, except Kuwait which ranked 97th. The strong gain maintained by the UAE suggests that procurement decisions in the country foster technological innovations.

ICTs

Ahmed (2005) and Ahmed and Al-Roubaie (2012) argue that technology development is embedded in a country's history, cultural values and attitudes. Therefore, attitude to ICTs could also have something to do with national culture. There is also enormous variety in the socioeconomic context of Arab countries, and a related large variability between them in terms of their current status with respect to ICTs, in areas such as their existing equipment base, the availability of trained personnel and their current levels of usage of IT/S.

According to the latest report by the International Telecommunication Union, entitled Measuring the Information Society Report 2014, UAE is the second top country in the Arab States in terms of the ICT Development Index (IDI). Moreover, UAE records the highest increase (largest improvements) in ranking, shooting up 14 places in IDI from 2012 to 2013, achieving a global ranking of 32.

All indicators included in the access sub-index showed improvement from 2011–2012. The report also states that mobile-cellular telephone penetration, in particular, rose by more than 14% to 170% in 2012. Moreover, the recent household survey conducted by the country's Telecommunication Regulatory Authority (TRA, 2012) states that virtually all residents use a mobile phone and that 85% of the population use the Internet regularly, for the most part through a high-speed connection. In the use sub-index, UAE registered great progress in the number of wireless-broadband subscriptions.

Also, according to the 2011 Digital Opportunity Index (DOI)[1] and WEF reports (2011), the UAE continues to lead the Arab world in the adoption of ICTs. It was expected to spend about US$3.3 billion on ICT hardware for schools, hospitals and other civil projects for the period 2008–2011. The index also reveals an alarming picture for many countries in the region, moving backward across the table from 2005–2011 world rankings. The ranking of rich countries, such as Kuwait (moved from 49th in 2005 to 60th in 2006) and Saudi Arabia (moved from 72nd place in 2005 to 75th place in 2006), shows that a nation's economic status does not always correspond to its path towards the information society.

Moreover, based on the most recent data from the World Bank Knowledge Assessment

---

[1] The DOI is a standard tool that governments, operators, development agencies, researchers and others can use to measure the digital divide and compare ICT performance within and across countries.

Methodology (www.worldbank.org/kam), UAE has reported the highest penetration rate of 2.1 telephones per 1000 population compared to all other GCC countries, Singapore and the Republic of Korea (see World Bank, 2008 and 2012). It also reported the highest rates of computers (330 per 1000 population) and Internet users (520 per 1000 population) among other GCC countries, but lower than Singapore (740 and 660 per 1000 population, respectively) and the Republic of Korea (580 and 760 per 1000 population, respectively).

CONCLUSIONS

This chapter has provided an in-depth analysis of the UAE's technological readiness and its capacity to compete in the global economy. Evidence has revealed a positive progression of the UAE in transitioning towards the innovation-driven stage. This has been characterised by a high performance macro-economic environment and a high-quality infrastructure, particularly in the ICT sector. However, several issues remain a concern and challenges remain to be addressed. In recent years, the country's economy has experienced slow technological readiness and negative trade trends in foreign technology transfer. It has also exhibited low investments in education and R&D activities and a lack of ability to absorb, adapt and create new technology and knowledge.

8

CHAPTER

ROADMAP TOWARDS UAE'S 2021 VISION

WASD

UAE'S OVERALL PERFORMANCE AS A KE

Using the World Bank's KAM, Table 8.1 presents the recent performance of selected Arab/ Muslim countries as illustrated by the World Bank's Knowledge Economy Index (KEI) 2012, including 146 economies across the world. Table 8.1 also compares the current performance (World Bank, 2012) with countries' KEI 2000 (see Ahmed and Al-Roubaie, 2012). It is therefore clear from the analysis below that the picture across most Arab/Muslim counties varies from economies with impressive progress towards knowledge-based economies, such as UAE, to economies with a large decrease in their KEI, such as Kuwait. According to the 2012 World Bank's KEI, UAE excelled in 2012 with remarkable improvements towards the knowledge-

Table 8.1	Arab/Muslim countries KEIs with large improvements and reversals, 2012		
Country	*KEI*	*Rank*	*Change**
Sweden	9.43	1	–
Economies with large improvements in KEI rankings since 2000			
United Arab Emirates	6.94	42	+6
Oman	6.14	47	+18
Saudi Arabia	5.96	50	+26
Tunisia	4.56	80	+9
Iran	3.91	94	+1
Algeria	3.79	96	+14
Pakistan	2.45	117	+5
Nigeria	2.2	119	+5
Yemen	1.92	122	+6
Sudan	1.48	138	+1
Economies with decreases in KEI rankings since 2000			
Bahrain	6.9	43	−2
Malaysia	6.1	48	−3
Qatar	5.84	54	−5
Kuwait	5.33	64	−18
Turkey	5.16	69	−7
Jordan	4.95	75	−18
Lebanon	4.56	81	−13
Egypt	3.78	97	−9
Morocco	3.61	102	−10
Syria	2.77	112	−1
Bangladesh	1.49	137	−3
Myanmar	0.96	145	−8

Source: World Bank (2012).

*Changes in KEI ranks from 2000.

based economy, has scored 6.94 and ranked 42nd in the world, and is leading the Arab and Muslim countries (see World Bank, 2012).

Figure 8.1 portrays UAE's performance in 1995 and 2009, measured using the KEI. It demonstrates the country's preparedness to compete in the global KE, benchmarked against its GCC neighbours and other selected countries; namely, Singapore and the Republic of Korea, who succeeded in making great strides in the transition to knowledge-based economies. Countries in Figure 8.1 above the 45° regression line have improved their 2009 performance on the KE indicators compared to 1995, and those below the line have slipped. Accordingly, the UAE, together with Qatar, demonstrated an improved performance in the KE ladder compared to 1995; both top the GCC list with a KEI of 6.73 as of the 2009 performance. This indicates a faster change of 0.81 for Qatar compared to 0.25 for the UAE (see Table 8.2).

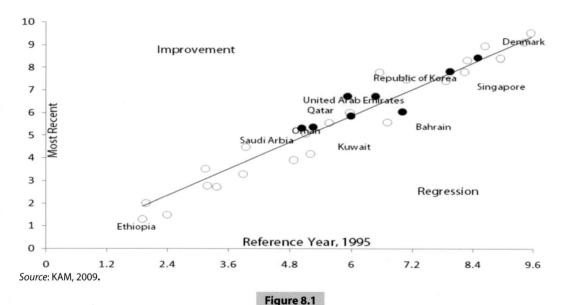

Source: KAM, 2009.

Figure 8.1

KEI for the UAE and selected countries (1995 and the most recent year)

Table 8.2 KEI for 1995 and the most recent year			
Country	KEI		
	Most recent	1995	Change
Singapore	8.44	8.49	−0.05
Republic of Korea	7.82	7.94	−0.12
Qatar	6.73	5.92	0.81
United Arab Emirates	6.73	6.48	0.25
Bahrain	6.04	7.00	−0.96
Kuwait	5.85	5.99	−0.14
Oman	5.36	5.25	0.11
Saudi Arabia (KSA)	5.31	5.03	0.28

Source: KAM, 2009.

Both countries, however, performed significantly lower than Singapore and the Republic of Korea. Benchmarked against 1995 KEI values, both Saudi Arabia and Oman have reported improved performance, reflecting a positive change of 0.28 and 0.11, respectively. The rest of the countries in the comparison group have shown varying levels of deterioration (negative change) in the KEI values, ranging from a minimum of 0.05 in Singapore to a maximum of 0.96 in Bahrain (Table 8.2).

A careful inspection of the four pillars of KE depicted in Table 8.3 and Figure 8.2; namely, economic incentive, education, innovation and ICT, reveals that the UAE has witnessed a significant upturn in the ICT sector in recent years. Matched with other GCC countries, the UAE ranked top in terms of the ICT knowledge component and efficient performance of innovation system of firms, as well as in the overall KI (see Table 8.3).

In economic incentives and institutional regime, UAE performed better than Saudi Arabia (KSA), stayed in the same line as Bahrain, but lagged behind Oman, Qatar and Singapore. The area where no real improvement (1995–2009) was shown is education (see Figure 8.2). Generally, UAE shows progressively satisfactory moves in the implementation of the KE pillars. The overall performance and development pattern in the key KE components, summarised by the KEI and the KI using recent KAM 2009 updated data, remained better than other GCC countries. However, the country shows a lower performance in the education pillar and is dropping behind the more dynamic economies of Singapore and the Republic of Korea in almost all KE indicators (see Table 8.3).

CONCLUSIONS AND POLICY RECOMMENDATIONS

Acknowledging the importance of stability and sustained economic growth, the UAE is seeking to achieve economic diversification and the transition to the KE. The country has had greater success in reducing dependency on oil as a dominant commodity compared to its GCC counterparts, and similar to developments made by Qatar.

Table 8.3 KEI, KI and the four pillars of the KE for the UAE, GCC and other countries for the most recent year

Index	UAE	Qatar	Bahrain	Kuwait	Oman	KSA	Korea	Singapore
KEI	6.73	6.73	6.04	5.85	5.36	5.31	7.82	8.44
KI	6.72	6.63	5.80	5.63	4.77	5.10	8.43	8.03
Economic Incentive and Institutional Regime	6.75	7.05	6.75	6.50	7.15	5.94	6.00	9.68
Education	4.90	5.37	5.82	4.93	4.47	4.89	8.09	5.29
Innovation	6.69	6.45	4.29	4.98	4.94	3.97	8.60	9.58
ICT	8.59	8.06	7.30	6.96	4.90	6.43	8.60	9.22

Source: World Bank (2012).

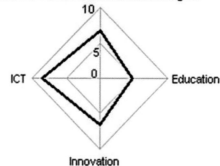

Comparison Group: **All Countries**   Type: **weighted**   Year: **most recent** (KAM 2009)

Source: KAM, 2009.

Figure 8.2

KEI of the four pillars for the UAE ,1995, and the most recent year, 2009

Economic diversification

The results from the data employed using the Hodrick-Prescott statistical technique when synchronising the manufacturing sector with the oil sector, reveals that 66.7% of output gaps in the two sectors have the same sign, signifying a high level of dependence of the manufacturing sector on the oil sector. However, as revealed by the trend analysis, this dependence is decreasing over time and the manufacturing sector is showing an independent growth away from the oil sector. This growth, however, is generally pushed by the growth of mainly labour-intensive activity and is therefore dependent on production processes that employ low technology levels.

Notably, UAE technology production is suffering a great deal as a result of the country's high dependence on imports of technology and technology products, creating a huge import-export balance of payments deficit. Nonetheless, trivial growth in technology exports has been reported recently (post-2000) and is mainly attributed to increasing development in the country's technological infrastructure, and insignificantly attributed to increased levels of inward Foreign Direct Investment (FDI).

Education system, skills and technological readiness

Evidence reveals a positive progression of the UAE in transitioning towards the innovation-driven stage, characterised by a high performance macro-economic environment and a high quality infrastructure, particularly in the ICT sector. However, several issues remain a concern and challenges remain to be addressed. In recent years, the country's economy experienced negative trade trends in foreign technology transfer, exhibited low investments in education and R&D activities and a lack of ability to absorb, adapt and create new technology and knowledge.

The UAE needs to increase its investment in education and R&D activities by increasing public expenditure, at least to match industrialised nations' minimum levels, and by encouraging more private sector contributions. Investment in the education and R&D sectors should be coupled with strategic reforms that ensure aligning learning and research outcomes to meet labour market demands and KE requirements. Particular focus should concentrate on strengthening technical and vocational training and revamping of curricula— particularly at the higher education level, where learning outcomes should emphasise the promotion of critical thinking skills, together with creativity and problem-solving capacities. This is instrumental in providing a highly skilled professional workforce to counteract the current mismatch in supply and demand in the country's human resources. It is also instrumental in providing the R&D manpower required to improve the country's ability to adapt and assimilate new technologies and to develop an innovation base. UAE investment in knowledge inputs would benefit the country's competitiveness standing and increase its chances of achieving sustained productivity growth as a result of increasing the indigenous innovation and the domestic value added of its goods and exports.

The UAE needs to emphasise more interaction and collaboration among all constituents in the R&D sector—including the government, the private sector and the wide pool of scientists and researchers in its universities and research institutions—in order to improve research efficiency and increase the size and quality of research output.

Overall, it is clear that the UAE's endeavours to join the KE club are supported by a well-established physical and communications infrastructure. It also has clear strategic objectives and priorities to diversify the economy away from the hydrocarbon-based economic activities.

UAE's commitment to transitioning to a KE is receiving the required political backing and is further supported by the availability of significant financial resources and wealth that can play a proactive part in realising the KE vision. The key to achieving sustainable economic growth and stability, however, hinges on the optimal utilisation of these assets in production and development, embracing the KE fundamentals and promoting entrepreneurship, innovation and global competitiveness.

CASE STUDY ANALYSIS

WASD

KNOWLEDGE MANAGEMENT FRAMEWORK (MUSHARAKA)

Department of Municipal Affairs (DMA), Government of Abu Dhabi

INTRODUCTION

In December 2009, one of the authors, Allam Ahmed, was appointed to lead Abu Dhabi Government (ADG) Department of Municipal Affairs (DMA) Major Knowledge Management Project, *first of its kind in Abu Dhabi and the Middle East: "Musharaka—Excellence through Knowledge.* This focuses on empowering employees, enabling them to improve the quality and efficiency of services provided to residents. Musharaka aims to enable employees to acquire and share information and international best practices, create creative and up-to-date methods for communication, exchange of knowledge and experiences, promote their functional performance, increase their productivity and enhance provided services. Musharaka is considered by the government of Abu Dhabi as a first of its kind transformation project, changing employees' culture in the government of Abu Dhabi.

DEPARTMENT OF MUNICIPAL AFFAIRS (DMA)

The vision of DMA is to create "an advanced municipal system that enables sustainable development and enhances quality of living for the Emirate of Abu Dhabi". The mission is to achieve ADG's objective of providing distinctive municipal services that enhance the quality of living of all residents through coordination, oversight and monitoring of the AD municipalities and municipal councils. The aim of DMA is to achieve the general policies of ADG by way of supervision and control over the municipal councils in Abu Dhabi (AD) concerned in providing such services.

DMA main customers are Abu Dhabi City Municipality (ADM), Al-Ain City Municipality (AAM) and Western Region Municipality (WRM), where DMA acts as a regulatory and supervisory body responsible for providing support for all municipalities and stakeholders. DMA also acts as the main body responsible for all new strategic initiatives and projects under the Executive Council of Abu Dhabi government. Various entities benefit from DMA's international expertise and consultancy, as well as its partnership and networking facilities

DMA organization structure (see Figure 9.1) comprised the following divisions:

- Local Governance, responsible for the municipal regulations, strategic support, Municipal Councils management and customer complaints.
- Municipal Support, responsible for municipal operations support, inter-department coordination and training.
- Property Registrar, responsible for handling complex property requests and transactions, and managing the Property Registrar database.
- DMA Support Services, responsible for providing administrative and legal support to the DMA.

MUSHARAKA

"Musharaka—Excellence through Knowledge" initiative is part of the municipal system efforts to achieve Abu Dhabi's 2030 vision, which aims for Abu Dhabi to be one of the top five governments in the world and one of the best places for living, working and investing. This strategic initiative is being launched in coordination with the General Secretariat of the Executive Council as part of Abu Dhabi Government's policy agenda of creating a comprehensive knowledge-based economy in the Emirate. Musharaka aims to encourage and enable employees from DMA and other municipalities to share knowledge and expertise in order to improve the quality of the delivered services.

The objectives of "Musharaka" are, therefore, to identify and capture useful and valuable knowledge; to classify and store knowledge; to deliver relevant knowledge in a simple, fast, efficient way and at the right time to relevant users; to maintain the Information Life Cycle through processes and policies; and to ensure information security through processes and policies. Figure 9.2 depicts an analysis and illustration of DMA cultural web.

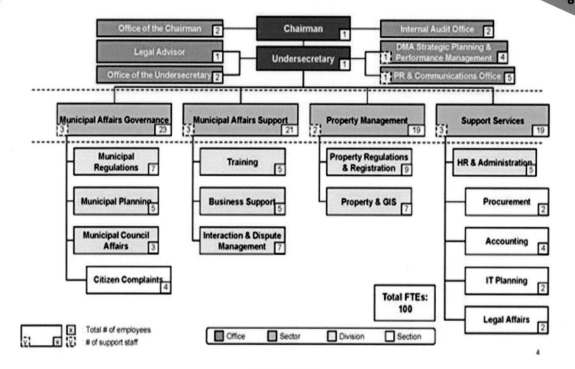

Figure 9.1

DMA organisation structure

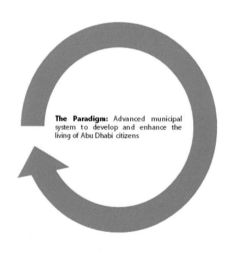

The Paradigm: Advanced municipal system to develop and enhance the living of Abu Dhabi citizens

· **Symbols:** DMA Logo including Abu Dhabi, Al Ain and Western Region Municipality (Tree), Open space offices for employees and closed for managers, Slogan used "Sharing knowledge making a difference"

· **Power structure:** Top management are the decision makers and the most effective people, If the is no buy-in from top management there will be no buy-in from the employees

· **Organization Structure:** Hierarchy (Top to Bottom), A cooperative organization

· **Control Systems:** Employees' performance appraisal, Employee of the month, KM champions have 10% evaluation from the KM office and 90% from his/her managers, Policies, Employees' handbook, 5 years strategic plan

· **Rituals and Routines:** Annual gathering, New employees' tour and induction, Ramadan gifts, Ramadan Iftar day, KM seminar day, Knowledge champions event every three months, Weekly brain teasers

· **Stories and Myths:** Management, Employees, Customers, Other municipal system entities, management and employees, Other organizations

Figure 9.2

DMA cultural web

Musharaka has three stages (see Figure 9.3) that include *assessing* current state, strategies and context, *designing* changes that will drive and support Knowledge Management and *implementing a Framework* across the DMA and Municipalities. In the first stage of the project we have identified and consulted with all key sponsors of Musharaka in DMA and other entities. Secondly we managed to create a guiding coalition of visible leadership and provide coaching and guidance for leaders and sponsors.

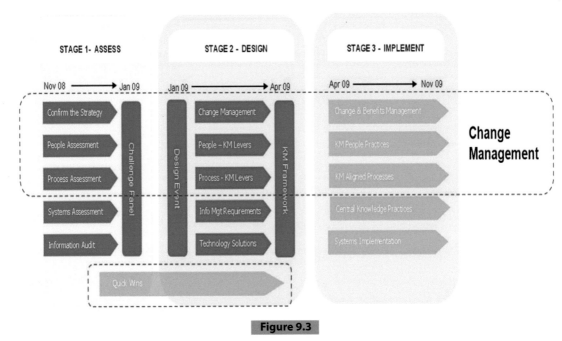

Figure 9.3

Musharaka's change management components

Technology roadmap

Musharaka framework includes four basic components, as shown in Figure 9.4, namely:

- Knowledge and Collaboration Portal;
- Enterprise Search and Semantic Middleware;
- Integration Middleware;
- Active Directory Integration.

The technology roadmap aims to highlight the various options that are essential for the expendability, extensibility and improvement of the KM system. The roadmap is an essential step into technological planning; it will outline products and tools used in the various service layers to deliver the short, medium and long term KM implementation strategies within the DMA and the other municipalities.

The roadmap aims to achieve the following benefits:

- Identify the desired KM system requirements;
- Identify the major technology areas of focus;
- Specify the technology drivers and their targets;

Detailed Framework Design

The DMA's KM Framework contains over 60 business, information and technology components designed in accordance with world-class practices:

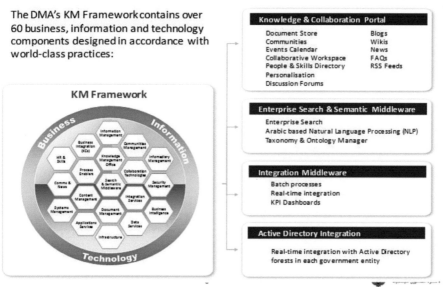

Figure 9.4

Musharaka detailed framework design

- Identify technology alternatives;
- Optimise and streamline technological development processes.

Musharaka portal

An internal portal (see Figure 9.5) has been created for the DMA and the municipalities to enhance employee communications. It also links and facilitates the work procedures in the DMA and the municipalities for the exchange of information in joint and secure mechanisms that can be easily accessed via the web link: http://musharaka. Moreover, during the project more than 40 employees, including KMOs, have been fully trained on the Musharaka portal.

Musharaka portal environment built upon Microsoft Windows SharePoint Services (WSS). WSS includes: use of templates for producing Web 2.0 features (WIKIs and BLOGs), publishing calendars, collaboration, email integration, task coordination, surveys, document collaboration, issue tracking, use of variants, search and search results, alerting, task notifications, RSS feeds provisioning, rights trimmed user interface, recycle bin, document libraries, large list and cross list indexing, metadata, content types, application templates, workflow, founded in ASP.net 2.0, performance caching, folders in lists, list indexing, cross-list queries, list items, property bags, web services, change logs, event receivers, job services, feature framework, solution deployment, version history, version tracking, pluggable authentication, Interoperability and integration.

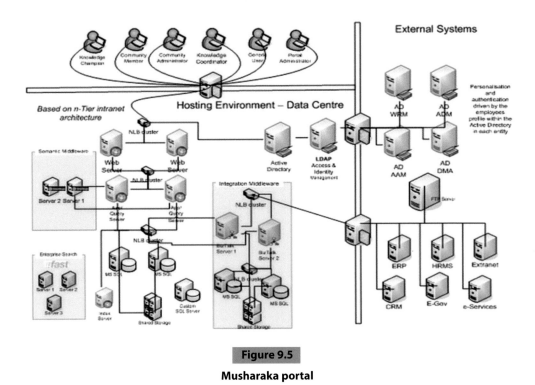

Figure 9.5

Musharaka portal

The KM system uses a number of SQL servers in a cluster setup. These servers manage and provide the necessary data storage for the portal and also the transactional storage for the BizTalk. BizTalk—generally classified as an enterprise service bus—is used as the integration middleware for the KM portal to enable the exchange of information and knowledge between KM and other third party systems. It is useful in transforming data and providing a mechanism for loose coupling of programming logic to events related to data moving/transforming from one location to another.

Information security

In the absence of a tailored information security policy within the DMA, it is not possible to conduct a full security audit on the KM system. The government security audit, as stipulated by Abu Dhabi Systems and Information Centre (ADSIC), is based on different types of controls and classified within the following groups:

- Core ADSIC Controls;
- Abu Dhabi Government Information Security Office (ADG-ISO) Controls;
- Entity Specific Controls.

At the moment, the only ADSIC-driven security audit can be implemented solely against the controls related to the Core ADSIC and ADG-ISO; this will not be effective as the majority of the controls are entity specific. DMA shall therefore develop and maintain an organization-specific information security policy that is supplemental to ADSIC's information security policy. DMA is therefore defining within the information security policy each of the critical security roles and responsibilities to be fulfilled by stakeholders in the information security processes. Moreover, DMA is planning for how the policy should be approved, reviewed and updated on a regular basis.

CHANGE MANAGEMENT AND LEADERSHIP ALIGNMENT

Understanding change

The success of a transformational project such as Musharaka depends on excellent, efficient and timely change management. This requires a good understanding of the change by the sponsors and leaders within the organisation, which will be achieved by ensuring that the sponsors and the leaders fully understand the following:

- What is the change?
- Why is the change important?
- What are the intended benefits?
- What are the risks associated with not managing the change?

One of the key roles of an effective change management team is to ensure that the sponsors and leaders have the answers to all these questions from the start of the project so that they feel confident acting as project champions when communicating with teams. Leadership support is vital to maintain ongoing success and it is essential that awareness levels are achieved across the entire organisation.

Organisational change refers to deliberate attempts to change one or more elements of the internal environment, such as technology or structure. Change in one element usually stimulates change in other areas. A change programme is therefore an attempt to change one or more aspects of the internal context, which then provides the context of future actions. The prevailing context can itself help or hinder change efforts.

As clearly demonstrated in Figure 9.3, the change management approach adopted in Musharaka sets the framework and direction for all change-related activities throughout the project.

The objectives of Musharaka change management plan include:

- *New ways of working*: To create an environment and support structure within each entity that will encourage positive changes in ways of working—in line with Musharaka requirements.
- *Communications*: To use appropriate communications and channels to ensure that each individual affected can understand what the project means for him/her, and how it can benefit him/her.
- *Influence*: To ensure that key leaders and stakeholders are influenced appropriately to gain their buy-in and help maximise the project's success.

- *Knowledge transfer*: To ensure that all necessary skills have been transferred to the KMOs in order to effectively manage Musharaka on an ongoing basis.
- *Resistance to change*: To work with the entities to help manage employees' resistance to change.
- *Continuous improvement*: To enable measurement and tracking of the benefits delivered by Musharaka, in order to drive performance and continued improvements.
- *Feedback*: To enable the project team to evolve the change management approach based on feedback: what works, and what doesn't work.

Managing change is critical to the success of Musharaka. The change management plan includes several major components that will be discussed in detail in what follows.

Scenario planning and readiness assessment

Musharaka scenario planning involves various activities started by a major design workshop for senior managers and staff to explore their own ideas about the municipal system in five years after the execution of Musharaka. The next step was to collect and analyse data about the current trends in KM. In doing so, DMA understood the existing information and KM activities undertaken within each of the entities, as well as KM leading practices in other government entities. Accordingly, stories were developed for all possible future scenarios and the implications of these different scenarios on the municipal system as well as the citizen of AD in the next ten years and also towards AD 2030 vision for the future were discussed. Moreover, the scenario planning has led to establishing four Knowledge Management Offices (KMOs) within all entities, as well as developing areas for focus that will form improvement opportunities in the design stage of Musharaka. Indicators needed to ensure that a scenario is happening have also been discussed and evaluated at the readiness stage.

Communicating change

Musharaka communication plan is designed to:

- Ensure timely and appropriate generation, collection, distribution, storage, retrieval and ultimate disposition of Musharaka project information.
- Provide the critical links among people and information that are necessary for successful communications.
- Guide the Musharaka project manager, project team, stakeholders, sponsors and everyone involved in the project to understand how communications affect the project as a whole.
- Ensure all relevant parties are aware of information related to all stages of Musharaka.
- Ensure the stakeholders experience awareness and engagement throughout the project journey.
- Provide a clear framework to build upon throughout the project and update based on feedback gained from the client and work streams.

Moreover the communication plan that follows the three stages of the project details the following: Communication; Audience; Format; Purpose; Channel; Timing and Ownership. Figure 9.6 lists all different communication channels used during the Musharaka project.

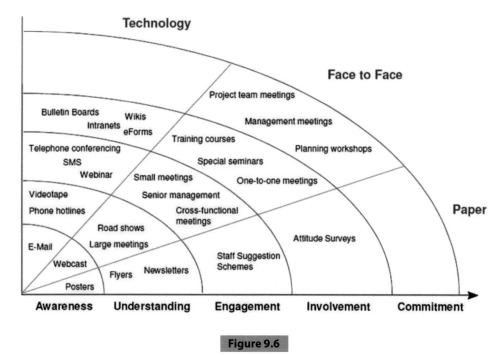

Figure 9.6

Musharaka communication channels

Given the importance of the employees' feedback during the entire project, the communication plan was evaluated and assessed on a continuous basis to ensure key questions were answered and that the level of commitment increased during the project. Evaluating feedback also enabled us to adapt our communication plan to meet the needs of employees at any given point in time, which would eventually result in continuous improvement for future communication. Figure 9.7 illustrates the importance of feedback and the commitment during the project.

Leadership alignment and stakeholder mapping

There is clear evidence that many transformation programmes fail because of a lack of clear leadership and sponsorship. Visible and timely leadership is therefore essential in times of change in the workplace. It is also is necessary to ensure that DMA leaders themselves do not become disenfranchised or threatened by the changes underway.

In the first stage of the project, we identified and consulted with all key sponsors of Musharaka in DMA and other entities. Secondly we managed to create a guiding coalition of visible leadership and provided coaching and guidance for leaders and sponsors. In doing so, leaders assembled a group with enough power to lead the change, encouraging that group to work as a team. These steps were coupled with full coordination of key interventions and gateway events. As a result of all these measures, we managed to ensure leaders inspired the change team and wider stakeholders, and backed it up with strategies to help achieve DMA vision. As a result, leaders used every vehicle possible we made available for them

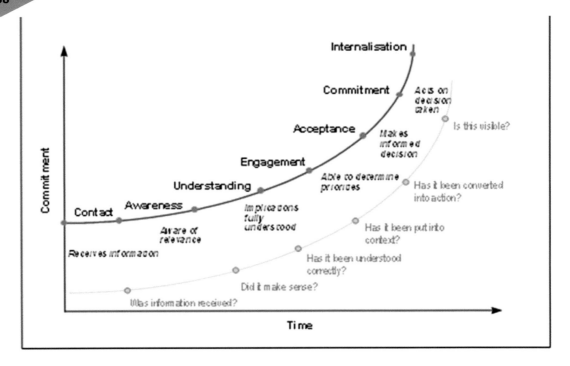

The importance of feedback

to communicate the new vision and strategies for making it happen, including their own behaviours. We also ensured that leaders understood the need to stay ahead of competition, and identified and discussed crises as well as opportunities.

Moreover, to support DMA internal and external leaders, stakeholders to enhance the success of the project, we used stakeholder mapping (see Figure 9.8) to analyse the initial level of support and influence of each stakeholder on Musharaka. Musharaka stakeholders included Steering Committee, Executive Directors, and Other UAE Government Entities etc. We also considered where we need stakeholders' interest and influence for the project success.

Leadership engagement guidelines

Key guidelines (Table 9.1) have been developed to provide guidance to each entity when managing leadership engagement throughout the Musharaka project.

The benefits of a structured leadership alignment initiative include:

- *Clarity of vision:* Starting with the top team but shared by the rest of DMA.
- *Improved results:* Both at a personal and at a team level—as the effort of individuals is better aligned with strategic objectives.
- *Reduction in wasted time:* At meetings, in terms of documents produced or activities conducted—as effort on non-critical activity is minimised.
- *Effective change that sticks:* Embedded in processes and able to survive any movement of personnel.

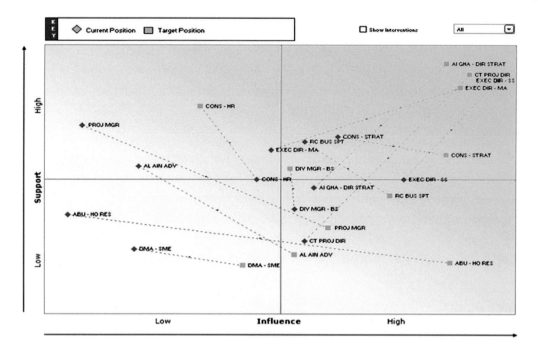

Figure 9.8

Musharaka stakeholder mapping

Table 9.1	Leadership engagement guidelines
Increase Leadership Presence	• Leadership should always attend Knowledge related events to endorse the importance e.g. Knowledge Champions Event. • Leadership should attend the KM system training • Leadership should be involved in a Community of Practice/Interest
Increase Leadership Communication	• All messages of awareness, expectations, standards and celebration should originate and be delivered by leadership. • Face to face communication over e-mails is preferred e.g. as part of the weekly team meeting there could be a slot for knowledge management activities.
Increase Leadership Alignment	• Ensure leaders are aligned and share a common compelling vision of Knowledge Management during Stage 3 of the project. • Ensure they are aware of the dependencies on their team in order to carry out some Knowledge Management activities. • Exec Directors must set specific expectations from their division managers with measureable objectives on KM contribution. These should also be enforced and measured regularly. • Ensure all leaders understand the key messages of the KM system and the change impacts on their divisions. • Leaders should have the relevant briefing materials they need to be able to support their employees with Knowledge Management.

- *Speeded-up decision-making:* More authority is delegated as greater numbers of people understand the key drivers, and decisions are made on an informed basis.
- *Improved morale:* Particularly at the level below the executive, who have additional understanding of both the "how" and the "why".

LEADING AND MANAGING THE KNOWLEDGE MANAGEMENT OFFICE

The first component of Musharaka was the establishment of specialised KMOs in the DMA and in each municipality to be part of a hub and spoke model to ensure consistency in standards and approach. Each entity's Knowledge Management Office (KMO) has been tailored to their needs to support Musharaka in their entity.

The main aims of the KMO are:

- Planning, communication and governance for all KM projects and initiatives.
- Maintaining standards and publishing content—good knowledge working.
- Encouraging and promoting knowledge sharing among all staff.
- Promoting knowledge sharing in each DMA division by appointed KM Champion.
- Assisting with design and implementation of KM initiatives
- Transition of KMO activities and skills from the international consultant to the KMO team.

Change agents – *Knowledge Champions (KC)*

Change agents are critical for the success or failure of any major transformation projects in the public sector, such as Musharaka. It is therefore important to understand the characteristics and competences of those change agents, as well as the approach and methodology they have to adopt in order to champion the change.

Each division in DMA and other entities have a change agent (referred to as Knowledge Champion in Musharaka) assigned throughout the project and post Go Live to be the main point of contact for all knowledge-related issues in their divisions and to act as a supporting colleague to the KMO team.

The roles and responsibilities of Musharaka knowledge champion include:

- Raising the profile of Musharaka.
- Helping his/her colleagues in the division to look for and provide good-quality knowledge items.
- Collecting knowledge items from his/her colleagues.
- Quality checking knowledge items.
- Coordinating Musharaka communications and events.
- Coaching and training staff within his/her business area.
- Implementing best practices and lessons learned within his/her area.

Knowledge transfer

The objectives of knowledge transfer are to ensure we can identify where the current skills do not meet Musharaka's requirements and to create a training and knowledge transfer programme that both develops those skills and persuades people to accept the new system. Also to ensure the necessary knowledge and skills are transferred from the international consultants and experts to various leaders in DMA and other municipalities, thus reducing longer-term consultancy dependency and costs, and raising the overall capability and capacity of DMA staff to deliver and maintain Musharaka.

Musharaka's key aspects of knowledge and skills transfer entails consultants using existing tools and methodologies built up from industry best practice and other client engagements to produce specific knowledge items for the DMA and municipalities. Once produced, these items will need to be handed over to the appropriate KMO leaders for ownership. And in order to achieve the objective of transferring knowledge from the international consultants to DMA staff, a specific amount of coaching to our DMA staff is expected from the consultants during the course of the project, particularly in stages 2 and 3. Skills transfer also involves spreading skills and experience through focused skills transfer activities, thereby leveraging the value added from the investment.

Moreover, appropriate training is also provided with specific instruction to DMA leadership team fully tailored and developed modules by the consultant. Finally a proper evaluation process was conducted to ensure the expectations around the level of knowledge and skills transfer (KST) will need to be defined up front. KST targets and evaluations have also be incorporated into performance appraisals and objectives of the identified individuals undergoing KST. However, the responsibility rest with the managers of these individuals to incorporate these targets with assistance from the consultant.

Managing employees' resistance to change

Resistance to change is considered an important factor in managing the design and implementation stages of Musharaka. The success of a transformational project such as Musharaka depends on excellent, efficient and timely dealing with employees' resistance to change. This requires a good understanding of the change by the sponsors and leaders within the organisation, which was achieved by ensuring that the sponsors and leaders fully understood the change, purpose, benefits and risks associated with not managing the change. In addition, it was essential to raise the awareness across the organization with the leadership support. Figure 9.9 provides the various steps undertaken during the project to deal with the resistance to change.

Moreover, the project established various Committees to ensure the smooth running of the project. Based on H. E., the Chairman of DMA's circular regarding the launch of Musharaka in DMA and municipalities, a Steering Committee (SC) has been established to supervise and steer the project in DMA and municipalities. The SC approved more than 60 components for the "Musharaka" system. Moreover, to support Musharaka, DMA established the Inter Coordination Group (ICG) Committee to provide all necessary support for the project. The ICG reviews all reports of the project and suggests all necessary recommendations for consideration by the SC.

A very thorough readiness assessment exercise was also undertaken at the early stages of the project, as well as various other critical activities. Also, the establishment Musharaka KMOs, various Communities of Practice (CoPs) to get more engagement among employees, conducting various awareness sessions, workshops and seminars, as well as recruiting many change agents (referred to as knowledge champions in Musharaka).

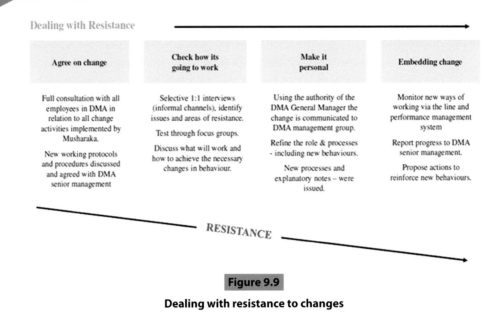

Figure 9.9

Dealing with resistance to changes

RESULTS AND BENEFITS OF MUSHARAKA

To increase engagement and awareness, we implemented a number of quick wins. Typically, these are relatively small initiatives with few dependencies that focus on delivering value to the customer. Moreover, to ensure we tracked the benefits delivered by the quick wins, we developed a performance framework to measure the longer term KPIs and benefits. Musharaka key benefits and outcomes:

For DMA and the municipal system

➢ Musharaka enhanced employee engagement, performance and productivity, and ultimately helped boost customer service.
➢ Musharaka addressed several of the ADG excellence criteria and helped DMA become a more excellent and modern municipal system.
➢ Musharaka positioned DMA as a KM pioneer with ADG, introducing practices and systems that were globally recognised as essential to support ambitious growth of services.

For the employee

➢ With greater access to knowledge, Musharaka allowed employees to do a better job and be recognised for their expert skills.
➢ As employees had better access to information, they became able to deliver services more efficiently and effectively to residents of the municipality.
➢ An online employee directory and vibrant Communities of Practice and Interest provided employees with a chance to develop relationships and to build and share their expertise across the municipalities.

And for the Emirate of Abu Dhabi, Musharaka enhanced municipal services, which in turn helped in making the Emirate of Abu Dhabi a better place to live, work and do business.
Musharaka achievements included:

➢ First government entity in Abu Dhabi to launch a complete Knowledge Management Framework (KM).
➢ Fulfilled a sub criterion of the Abu Dhabi Award for Excellence in Government Performance:
  a. *Submission for the ADG Excellence award for KM category four.*
  b. *Thoroughly reviewed by Abu Dhabi Award for Excellence Office to be presented before General Secretariat of the Executive Council as a model for the entire ADG KM.*
  c. *Several appreciation letters and request to access Musharaka from various government entities, including the Prime Minister Office.*
  d. *Selected by a Lecturer from Zayed University for her PhD Case Study at the University of Birmingham, UK.*

➢ Only entity from across ADG presented during the United Nations World Conference on ICTs & Development, Abu Dhabi 5th December 2010.
➢ Selected as one of the top five case studies in terms of change management in the world by the Association of Change Management Professionals, United States, 2010.
➢ Completed live deployment of Musharaka System (KM Portal & Intranet) in all municipalities on 12 Jan 2011.
➢ Completed full and first in AD KM training on 23 Dec 2010 for more than 40 employees from across municipalities.
➢ Completed User Acceptance Test (UAT) on 8 Dec 2010 for the Musharaka system by all KMOs across municipalities.
➢ 60 components agreed by the SC and included in the system.
➢ Establishment of more than 20 Communities of Practices across all municipalities and total of over 500 members (receiving communities joining requests on a daily basis).
➢ 150 Knowledge Champions actively involved in KM across all municipalities.
➢ Four Knowledge Champions Events organised across all municipalities attended by more than 1000 employees in the municipal system and other AD entities.
➢ Three Operational KPIs recommended and agreed. The first KPI submitted to SPPM third Quarter 2011.
➢ Three processes recommended and agreed with BPR project.
➢ More than 75 awareness sessions conducted across municipalities and attended by more than 2000 municipal staff.
➢ Ten quick wins projects completed successfully across municipalities.
➢ More than 9000 valid knowledge documents have been uploaded and shared across the Municipal System.
➢ Providing nine e-services for employees (Out of twelve—toward centric employees' self-service gateway).

- ➤ Shared more than 220 news updates across the Municipal System activities via Musharaka News Hub.
- ➤ Eleven KM seminars attended by more than 2500 staff from DMA, municipalities as well as almost 40 entities (public and private) from across UAE.
- ➤ Musharaka system enhancement before the end-user feedback.
- ➤ Promote the DMA and the KM initiative across ADG.

Performance measurement and feedback

Measurement of change management performance throughout the Musharaka project will allow the team to demonstrate value provided by the Change Management activities, identify areas of concern among the stakeholders and provide useful data to Musharaka work stream leads, while managing the successful delivery of the project. Measurement of change management also allowed the leaders to celebrate Musharaka successes; correct actions whenever required; explain results and performance to various stakeholders; build a comprehensive story of the change, enhancing team member satisfaction; justify future initiatives and compile "Lessons Learned" and improve future change projects.

Put simply, "Performance Management" is about knowing what the organisation is trying to achieve, developing effective ways of delivering on priorities, knowing that we are achieving high standards and looking at how to improve. This is important on Musharaka, as DMA needs to ensure that all the processes we design will deliver value and that this value can be demonstrated. As part of the design stage, we will be capturing benefits and Key Performance Indicators (KPIs), and developing a benefits tracker to monitor these.

There are many ways, including both quantitative and qualitative, to measure the success of the activities. Methods adopted in Musharaka include Interviews; Surveys; Focus Groups; and Issues and Risks. The change management team progress checklist (Table 9.2) is used as tool to provide an understanding of how well the change process is going on and what the team change need to do to improve (*3: Good, 2: Average, 1: Poor*).

Table 9.2	Musharaka change management team progress checklist			
Questions		Score		
		1	2	3
Action plan	How are we doing against the plan?			
	How do we rate our successes so far?			
	To what degree are we achieving the desired impact?			
	How would we rate our access to resources?			
Commitment	How would we describe the level of sponsorship and support from leaders?			
	How would we rate the level of commitment from Musharaka client team?			
	How are we performing against deadlines?			
Excitement	How are the client project teams enthusiasm and commitment?			
	What level of personal enthusiasm so our project sponsor and change leaders demonstrate?			
	How well is the excitement communicated through words and action?			
Integration	How well are the change initiatives integrated with other change initiatives?			
	How well is the project integrated with change components? (workforce alignment, learning and development and performance management?			
	How well are we addressing the consequences of the project on the organisation's management processes? (staffing, rewards, measurements, comms, structure)			
Learning from experience	How successful are we at sharing project learnings and best practices throughout the project?			
	To what degree are team members developing professionally as a result of their experience?			

REFERENCES

WASD

REFERENCES

Abdalla Alfaki, I.M. and Ahmed, A. (2013) 'Technological readiness in the United Arab Emirates towards global competitiveness', *World Journal of Entrepreneurship, Management and Sustainable Development (WJEMSD)*, Vol. 9, No. 1, pp.4–13.

Abdalla, I., Al Waqfi, M., Harb, N., Hijazi, R. and Zoubeidi, T. (2008) 'Study of Dubai labor market: summary of main results', *Paper Presented at the 9th Annual Research Conference of the UAEU*, Al-Ain, UAE.

Abdalla, I., Al-Waqfi, M., Harb, N., Hijazi, R. and Zoubeidi, T. (2010) 'Labour policy and determinants of employment and wages in a developing economy with labour shortage', *LABOUR: Review of Labour Economics and Industrial Relations*, Vol. 24, No. 2, pp.163–177.

Abou-Zeid, E-S. (2002) 'A knowledge management reference model', *Journal of Knowledge Management*, Vol. 6, No. 5, pp.486–499.

Abu Dhabi Council for Economic Development (ADCED). (2012) *Abu Dhabi's Economic Performance in the Last 10 years, Chart Book (2001–2010)*, Available at: http://www.adced.ae/uploads/Chartbook.pdf.

ADG Statistical Centre (2011) Abu Dhabi, UAE.

Ahmed, A. (2005) 'Digital publishing and the new era of digital divide', *International Journal of Learning and Intellectual Capital*, Vol. 2, No. 4, pp.321–338.

Ahmed, A. and Al-Roubaie, A. (2012) 'Building a knowledge-based economy in the Muslim world: the critical role of innovation and technological learning', *World Journal of Science, Technology and Sustainable Development*, Vol. 9, No. 2, pp.76–98.

Ahmed, A. and Nwagwu, W. (2006) 'Challenges and opportunities of e-learning networks in Africa', *Development*, Vol. 49, No. 2, pp.58–64.

Ahn, J.H. and Chang, S.G. (2004) 'Assessing the contribution of knowledge to business performance: the KP3 methodology', *Decision Support Systems*, Vol. 36, No. 4, pp.403–416.

Al Awad, M. (2010) 'The cost of foreign labor in the United Arab Emirates', *Working paper No. 3, Institute for Social & Economic Research*, Zayed University, Abu Dhabi, July, Available at: www.ISER.ae, Accessed on November 2012.

Alavi, M. and Leidner, D.E. (1999) 'Knowledge management systems: issues, challenges and benefits', *Communications of AIS*, No. 1, p.7.

Alavi, M. and Leidner, D.E. (2001) 'Review: knowledge management and knowledge management systems: conceptual foundations and research issues', *MIS Quarterly*, Vol. 25, No. 1, pp.107–136.

Ali, A. (1996) 'Organizational development in the Arab World', *Journal of Management Development*, Vol. 15, No. 5, pp.4–21.

Al-Yahya, K. and Farah, S. (2009) 'Knowledge management in public sector: global and regional comparison', *Paper Presented to the International Conference on Administrative Development: Towards Excellence in Public Sector Performance*, Riyadh, 1–4 November.

American Productivity and Quality Center (APQC) (2000) 'Chevron Corporation', *Successfully Implementing Knowledge Management (Best Practices Report)*, 6 June 2000.

An, X., Deng, H., Wang, Y. and Chao, L. (2013) 'An integrated model for effective knowledge management in Chinese organizations', *Program: Electronic Library and Information Systems*, Vol. 47, No. 3, pp.320–336.

Armenakis, A.A. and Bedeian, A.G. (1999) 'Organizational change: a review of theory and research in the 1990's', *Journal of Management*, Vol. 25, No. 3, pp.293–315.

Aubert, J.E. and Reiffers, J.L. (2003) *Knowledge Economies in the Middle East and North Africa: Toward New Development Strategies*, The International Bank for Reconstruction and Development/The World Bank, Washington, DC.

Bachellerie, I.J. (2010) 'Knowledge creation and diffusion: the role of UAE universities', *Gulf Research Center (GRC), Report, Paper Presented to the WAITRO 20th Biennial Congress: Leadership for innovation*, DIT Dubai, Dubai, 13–14 October.

Baird, L., Henderson, J.C. and Watts, S. (1997) 'Learning from action: an analysis of the Center for Army Lessons Learned (CALL)', *Human Resource Management*, Vol. 36, No. 4, pp.385–395.

Barnes, S. (2002) *Knowledge Management System*, Thomson, p.181.

Barrett, D.J. (2002) 'Change communication: using strategic employee communication to facilitate major change', *Corporate Communications: An International Journal*, Vol. 7, No. 4, pp.219–231.

Bartholomew, S. (1997) 'The globalization of technology: a socio-cultural perspective', in J. Howells and J. Michie (Eds.). *Technology, Innovation and Competitiveness*, Cheltenham: Edward Elgar, pp.37–64.

Basher, S. (2010) 'Has the non-oil sector decoupled from the oil sector? A case study of Gulf Cooperation Council Countries', MAPRA, Munich Personal RePEc Archive, Paper No. 21059, posted 02. March 2010/07:32, Available at: http://mpra.ub.uni-muenchen.de/21059/.

Beazley, H., Boenisch, J. and Harden, D.G. (2002) *Continuity Management: Preserving Corporate Knowledge and Productivity when Employees Leave*, J. Wiley & Sons.

Becerra-Fernandez, I. and Sabherwal, R. (2001) 'Organizational knowledge management: a contingency perspective', *Journal of Management Information Systems*, Vol. 18, No. 1, pp.23–55.

Blackman, D.A. and Lee-Kelly, L. (2006) 'The role of human resource development in preventing organisational stagnation', *Management Decision*, Vol. 44, No. 5, pp.628–643.

Bosua, R. and Venkitachalam, K. (2013) 'Aligning strategies and processes in knowledge management: a framework', *Journal of Knowledge Management*, Vol. 17, No. 3, pp.331–346.

Brown, A. (1998) *Organisational Culture*, London: FT Pitman Publishing, pp.1–40.

Brown, K., Waterhouse, J. and Flynn, C. (2003) 'Change management practices – Is a hybrid model a better alternative for public sector agencies?' *The International Journal of Public Sector Management*, Vol. 16, No. 3.

Buniyamin, N. and Barber, K.D. (2004) 'The intranet: a platform for knowledge management system based on knowledge mapping', *International Journal of Technology Management*, Vol. 28, Nos. 7/8, pp.729–746.

Butler, T. (2003) 'From data to knowledge and back again: understanding the limitations of KMS', *Knowledge and Process Management*, Vol. 10, No. 3, pp.144–155.

Cao, Q., Thompson, M.A. and Triche, J. (2013) 'Investigating the role of business processes and knowledge management systems on performance: a multi-case study approach', *International Journal of Production Research*, Vol. 51, No. 18, pp.5565–5575.

Change, C-M., Hsu, M-H. and Yen, C-H. (2012) 'Factors affecting knowledge management success: the fit perspective', *Journal of Knowledge Management*, Vol. 16, No. 6, pp.847–861.

Chen, D.H.C. and Dahlman, C.J. (2006) *The Knowledge Economy, KAM Methodology and World Bank Operations*, Paper No. 35867, Washington, DC: World Bank.

Chen, J., Sun, P.Y.T. and McQueen, R.J. (2010) 'The impact of national cultures on structured knowledge transfer', *Journal of Knowledge Management*, Vol. 14, No. 2, pp.228–242.

Chiu, C.M., Hsu, M.H. and Wang, T.G. (2006) 'Understanding knowledge sharing in virtual communities: an integration of social capital and social cognitive theories', *Decision Support Systems*, Vol. 42, No. 3, pp.1872–1888.

Choi, B. and Lee, H. (2002) 'Knowledge management strategy and its link to knowledge creation process', *Expert Systems with Applications*, Vol. 23, No. 3, pp.173–187.

Chua, A.Y.K. and Banerjee, S. (2013) 'Customer knowledge management via social media: the case of Starbucks', *Journal of Knowledge Management*, Vol. 17, No. 2, pp.237–249.

Clark, P. (1989) 'Trend reversion in real output and unemployment', *Journal of Econometrics*, Vol. 40, pp.15–32.

Claver-Cortés, E., Zaragoza-Sáez, P. and Pertusa-Ortega, P. (2007) 'Organizational structure features supporting knowledge management processes', *Journal of Knowledge Management*, Vol. 11, No. 4, pp.45–57.

Cogley, T. and Nason, J. (1995) 'Effects of the Hodrick-Prescott filter on trend and difference stationary time series: implications of business-cycle research', *Journal of Economic Dynamics and Control*, Vol. 146, pp.155–178.

Collison, C. and Parcell, G. (2004) *Learning to Fly: Practical Knowledge Management from Leading and Learning Organisations*, Chichester: Capstone Publishing Ltd.

Cornell University, INSEAD and WIPO (2014) *The Global Innovation Index 2014. The Human Factor in Innovation, Fontainebleau, Ithaca, and Geneva*, ISSN 2263-3693, ISBN 978-2-9522210-6-1.

Damodaran, L. and Olphert, W. (2000) 'Barriers and facilitators to the use of knowledge management systems', *Behaviour and Information Technology*, Vol. 19, No. 6, pp.405–413.

Danofsky, S. (2005) *Open Access for Africa: Challenges, Recommendations and Examples*, United Nations ICT Task Force Working Group on the Enabling Environment, The United Nations Information and Communication Technologies Task Force, New York, USA.

Darroch, J. (2005) 'Knowledge management, innovation and firm performance', *Journal of Knowledge Management*, Vol. 9, No. 3, pp.101–115.

Davenport, T. and Prusak, L. (1998) *Working Knowledge: How Organizations Manage What They Know*, Boston, MA: Harvard Business Press.

De Gooijer, J. (2000) 'Designing a knowledge management performance framework', *Journal of Knowledge Management*, Vol. 4, No. 4, pp.303–310.

De Pablos, P.O. (2002) 'Knowledge management and organizational learning: typologies of knowledge strategies in the Spanish manufacturing industry from 1995 to 1999', *Journal of Knowledge Management*, Vol. 6, No. 1, pp.52–62.

Desouza, C. and Awazu, Y. (2006) 'Engaging tensions of knowledge management control', *Singapore Management Review*, Vol. 28, No. 1, pp.1–13.

Dixon, R. (1991) *Management Theory and Practice*, Oxford: Butterworth-Heinemann Ltd.

Doyle, M., Claydon, T. and Buchannan, D. (2000) 'Mixed results, lousy process: the management experience of organisational change', *British Journal of Management*, Vol. 11, pp.59–80.

Drucker, P. (1998) 'The coming of the new organization', *Harvard Business Review*, January–February, pp.45–53.

Dubai Statistics Center (2012) *Statistical Year Book*, Dubai Statistics Center, Available at: http://www.dsc.gov.ae/EN/Themes/Pages/Reports.aspx?TopicId=4&Year=2012.

Dufour, Y. and Steane, P. (2007) 'Implementing knowledge management: a more robust model', *Journal of Knowledge Management*, Vol. 11, No. 6, pp.68–80.

Fasano, U. and Iqbal, Z. (2003) 'GCC countries: from oil dependence to diversification', Washington: International Monetary Fund, Available at: http://www.imf.org/external/pubs/ft/med/2003/eng/fasano/index.htm.

Fiol, M.C. and Lyles, M.A. (1985) 'Organizational learning', *Academy of Management Review*, Vol. 10, No. 4, pp.803–813.

Flynn, N. (2007) *Public Sector Management*, 5th Edition, London: SAGE Publications.

Fontaine, M. and Lesser, E. (2002) *Challenges in Managing Organizational Knowledge*, IBM Institute for Knowledge-Based Organizations, IBM Corporation, IBM Global Services, New York, USA. This article was originally published in Next Frontier by World at Work and IHRIM (see www.worldatwork.org and www.ihrim.com).

Garvin, D.A. (1993) 'Building a learning organization', *Harvard Business Review*, Vol. 71, No. 4, July–August, pp.78–91.

Gebba, T.R. (2013) 'The role of governance in planning and implementing knowledge management strategy in the UAE: the case of RTA', *International Journal of Business Research and Development*, Vol. 2, No. 4, pp.1–26.

Ghoshal, S., Lampel, J., Mintzberg, H. and Quinn, J.B. (2003) *The Strategy Process*, 4th Edition, FT Prentice Hall.

Global Competitiveness Reports (GCR) (2006–2015) published by the World Economic Forum within the framework of the Global Benchmarking Network, Geneva, Available at: www.weforum.org/gcr, Accessed on 18 November 2013.

Haberberg, A. and Reiple, A. (2008) *Strategic Management: Theory and Application*, Oxford University Press.

Hamel, J.L. (2005) 'Knowledge for sustainable development in Africa towards new policy initiatives', *World Review of Science, Technology and Sustainable Development*, Vol. 2, No. 3, pp.217–229.

Handy, C. (1989) *The Age of Unreason*, London: Arrow.

Handzic, M. (2011) 'Integrated socio-technical knowledge management model: an empirical evaluation', *Journal of Knowledge Management*, Vol. 15, No. 2, pp.19–211.

Hansen, M.T. (2002) 'Knowledge networks: explaining effective knowledge sharing in multiunit companies', *Organization Science*, Vol. 13, No. 3, pp.232–248.

Hansen, M.T., Nohria, H. and Tierney, T. (1999) 'What's your strategy for managing knowledge?', *Harvard Business Review*, Vol. 77, No. 2, pp.106–116.

Haslinda, A. and Sarinah, A. (2009) 'A review of knowledge management models', *The Journal of International Social Research*, Vol. 2, No. 9.

Harvey, A. and Jaeger, A. (1993) 'Detrending, stylized facts and the business cycle', *Journal of Applied Econometrics*, Vol. 8, pp.231–247.

He, W. and Wei, K-K. (2009) 'What drives continued knowledge sharing? An investigation of knowledge-contribution and -seeking beliefs', *Decision Support Systems*, Vol. 46, No. 4, pp.826–838.

Heisig, P. (2009) 'Harmonisation of knowledge management: comparing 160 KM frameworks around the globe', *Journal of Knowledge Management*, Vol. 13, No. 4, pp.4–31.

Henderson, J.C., Sussman, S.W. and Thomas, J.B. (1997) 'Creating and exploiting knowledge for fast-cycle organizational response: the center for army lessons learned', *Advances in Applied Business Strategy*, Vol. 5, No. 4, pp.103–128.

Heracleous, L. and Johnston, R. (2009) 'Can business learn from the public sector?', *European Business Review*, Vol. 21, No. 4, pp.373–379.

Herschel, R., Nemati, H. and Steiger, D. (2001) 'Managing the tacit to explicit knowledge conversion problem: knowledge exchange protocols managing the tacit knowledge problem', *Journal of Knowledge Management*, Vol. 5, No. 1, pp.107–116.

Herschel, R. and Nemati, H. (2000) 'Chief knowledge officer: critical success factors for knowledge management', *Information Strategy: The Executive's Journal*, Vol. 16, No. 4, pp.37–45.

Hesson, M. (2007) 'Business process reengineer in UAE public sector; a naturalisation and residency case study', *Business Process Management*, Vol. 13, No. 5, pp.707–727.

Hijazi, R., Zoubeidi, T., Abdalla, I., Al-Waqfi, M. and Harb, N. (2008) 'A study of the UAE higher education sector in light of Dubai's strategic objectives', *Journal of Economic and Administrative Sciences*, Vol. 24, No. 1, pp.68–81.

Hofstede, G. (1994) *Cultures and Organizations*, London: Harper Collins.

Holsapple, C.W. and Joshi, K.D. (2002) 'Knowledge management: a threefold framework', *Information Society*, Vol. 18, No. 1, pp.47–64.

Hsu, M.H., Ju, T.L., Yen, C.H. and Chang, C.M. (2007) 'Knowledge sharing behavior in virtual communities: the relationship between trust, self-efficacy, and outcome expectations', *International Journal of Human-Computer Studies*, Vol. 65, No. 2, pp.153–169.

Huber, G.P. (1991) 'Organizational learning: the contributing processes and the literatures', *Organization Science*, February, pp.88–115.

Huczynski, A. and Buchanan, D. (2006) *Organizational Behaviour: An Introductory Text*, 6th Edition, London: Prentice Hall.

Hughes, M. (2010) *Resistance to Change*, [Workshop Notes] Brighton: University of Brighton Business School, unpublished.

Husain, A.M., Tazhibayeva, K. and Ter-Marirosyan, A. (2008) 'Fiscal policy and economic cycles in oil-exporting countries', *IMF Working Paper 08/253*, Washington: International Monetary Fund.

Hylton, A. (2003) *Why the Knowledge Audit is in Danger*, White Paper, October, Available at: http://www.annHylton.com.

International Monetary Fund (IMF) (2004) 'United Arab Emirates: 2004 Article IV consultation—staff report; public information notice on the executive board discussion; and statement by the executive director for the United Arab Emirates', *IMF Country Report* No. 04/175, International Monetary Fund Washington, DC.

Jimenez-Jimenez, D. and Sanz-Valle, R. (2013) 'Studying the effect of HRM practices on the knowledge management process', *Personnel Review*, Vol. 42, No. 1, pp.28–49.

Johnson, G., Scholes, K. and Whittington, R. (2005) *Exploring Corporate Strategy: Text and Cases*, 7th Edition, FT Prentice Hall.

Joshi, K.D., Sarker, S. and Sarker, S. (2007) 'Knowledge transfer within information systems development teams: examining the role of knowledge source attributes. Emerging issues in collaborative commerce', *Decision Support Systems*, Vol. 43, No. 2, pp.322–335.

Juma, M.N. (2003) 'The African virtual university. Challenges and prospects', in M. Beebe, B.O. Oyeyinka, K.M. Kouakpou and M. Rao (Eds.). *AfricaDotEdu. IT Opportunities and Higher Education in Africa*, New Delhi: Tata McGraw Hill.

KAMCO Research (2011) *UAE Economic Brief and Outlook 2011*, KAMCO Investment Research Department, Kuwait, Available at: http://www.kamconline.com.

Kankanhalli, A., Tan, B.C.Y. and Wei, K.K. (2005) 'Contributing knowledge to electronic knowledge repositories: an empirical investigation', *MIS Quarterly*, Vol. 29, No. 1, pp.113–143.

Keeble, D. and Wilkinson, F. (Eds) (2000) *High Technology Clusters, Networking and Collective Learning in Europe,* Aldershot: Ashgate.

Kettinger, W.J. and Li, Y. (2010) 'The infological equation extended: towards conceptual clarity in the relationship between data, information and knowledge', *European Journal of Information Systems*, Vol. 19, pp.409–421.

Kim, G., Yu, H. and Lee, H. (2003) 'Knowledge strategy planning: methodology and case', *Expert Systems with Applications*, Vol. 24, No. 3, pp.295–307.

Lai, H. and Chu, T. (2000) 'Knowledge management: a review of theoretical frameworks and industrial cases', *Proceedings of the 33rd Hawaii International Conference on System Sciences*, Hawaii.

Lee, C-F., Tsai, S.D-H. and Amjadi, M. (2012) 'The adaptive approach: reflections on knowledge management models', *Journal of Management Inquiry*, Vol. 21, No. 1, pp.30–41.

Lee, H. and Choi, B. (2003) 'Knowledge management enablers, processes, and organizational performance: an integrative view and empirical examination', *Journal of Management Information Systems*, Vol. 20, No. 1, pp.179–228.

Lefrere, P. (2007) 'Competing higher education futures in a globalizing world', *European Journal of Education*, Vol. 42, No. 2, pp.201–212.

Leonard, D. and Sensiper, S. (1998) 'The role of tacit knowledge group innovation', *California Management Review*, Vol. 40, No. 3, pp.112–132.

Liebowitz, J. (2003) 'Aggressively pursuing knowledge management over 2 years: a case study at a US government organization', *Knowledge Management Research and Practice*, Vol. 1, No. 2, pp.69–76.

Lin, T-C. and Huang, C-C. (2008) 'Understanding knowledge management system usage antecedents: an integration of social cognitive theory and task technology fit', *Information and Management*, Vol. 45, No. 6, pp.410–417.

Linderman, K., Schroeder, R.G., Zaheer, S., Liedtk, C. and Choo, A.S. (2004) 'Integrating quality management practices with knowledge creation processes', *Journal of Operations Management*, Vol. 22, No. 6, pp.589–607.

Liss, K. (1999) 'Do we know how to do that? Understanding knowledge management', *Harvard Management Update*, February, pp.1–4.

Lynch, R. (2003) *Corporate Strategy*, 3rd Edition, FT Prentice Hall.

Mabery, M.J., Gibbs-Scharf, L. and Bara, D. (2013) 'Communities of practice foster collaboration across public health', *Journal of Knowledge Management*, Vol. 17, No. 2, pp.226–236.

Malhotra, Y. (2004) 'Why knowledge management systems fail? Enablers and constraints of knowledge management in human enterprises', in E. Michael, D. Koenig and T. Kanti Srikantaiah (Eds.). *Knowledge Management Lessons Learned: What Works and What Doesn't*, Information Today Inc., *American Society for Information Science and Technology Monograph Series*, pp.87–112.

Mansell, R. and Wehn, U. (1998) *Knowledge Societies: Information Technology for Sustainable Development*, UN Commission on Science and Technology for Development, New York, NY: Oxford University Press Inc.

Manville, B. and Foote, N. (1996) 'Strategy as if knowledge mattered', *Fast Company*, April/May, p.66.

Margaryan, A., Milligan, C. and Littlejohn, A. (2011) 'Validation of Davenport's classification structure of knowledge-intensive processes', *Journal of Knowledge Management*, Vol. 15, No. 4, pp.568–581.

Maria, R.L. and Yi-Chen, L. (2011) 'Toward a unified knowledge management model for SMEs', *Expert Systems with Applications*, Vol 38, No. 1, pp.729–735.

Marr, B. and Creelman, J. (2011) *More With Less – Maximising Value in the Public Sector*, New York: Palgrave Macmillan.

Massingham, P. (2010) 'Knowledge risk management: a framework', *Journal of Knowledge Management*, Vol. 14, No. 3, pp.464–485.

McGlennon, D. (2006) 'Building research capacity in the gulf cooperation council countries: strategy, funding and engagement, UNESCO forum on higher education, research and knowledge', 29 November–01 December, Available at: http://portal.unesco.org/education/es/files/51665/1163495 3625McGlennonEN.pdf/McGlennon-EN.pdf, Accessed on July 2012.

McQueen, R. (1998) 'Four views of knowledge and knowledge management', *Proceedings of the Fourth Americas Conference on Information Systems*.

Mellahi, K. (2003) 'National culture and management practices: the case of Gulf Cooperation Council Countries', in M. Tayeb (Ed.). *International Management: Theories and Practices*, pp.87–105.

Mink, M., Jaccob, J. and Haan, J. (2007) 'Measuring synchronicity and comovement of business cycles with an application to the euro area', *CESifo Working Paper 2112*.

Molina, L.M., Montes, F.J.L. and Fuentes, M.D.M. (2004) 'TQM and ISO 9000 effects on knowledge transferability and knowledge transfers', *Total Quality Management and Business Excellence*, Vol. 15, No. 7, pp.1001–1015.

Muysken, J. and Nour, S. (2006) 'Deficiencies in education and poor prospects for economic growth in the Gulf Countries: the case of the UAE', *Journal of Development Studies*, Vol. 42, No. 6, pp.957–980.

Nan, N. (2008) 'A principal-agent model for incentive design in knowledge sharing', *Journal of Knowledge Management*, Vol. 12, No. 3, pp.101–113.

Nayir, D.Z. and Uzunçarsili, U. (2008) 'A cultural perspective on knowledge management: the success story of Sarkuysan company', *Journal of Knowledge Management*, Vol. 12, No. 2, pp.141–155.

Nonaka, I. (1994) 'A dynamic theory of organizational knowledge creation', *Organization Science*, Vol. 5, No. 1, pp.14–37.

Nonaka, I. (1998) 'The knowledge creating company', *Harvard Business Review on Knowledge Management*, pp.25–30.

Nonaka, I. and Takeuchi, H. (1995) *The Knowledge-Creating Company*, New York: Oxford University Press.

Nour, S.O.M. (2005) 'Science and technology development indicators in the Arab region: a comparative study of gulf and Mediterranean Arab Countries', *Discussion Paper Series No. 2005-3*, United Nations University, Institute for New Technologies, Maastricht, Available at: www.science.net/Docs/science%20in%20arab%20countries.pdf, Accessed on September 2012.

O'Leary, D.E. (2008) 'A multilingual knowledge management system: a case study of FAO and WAICENT', *Decision Support Systems*, Vol. 45, No. 3, pp.641–661.

OPEC – Organization of the Petroleum Exporting Countries (2013) *OPEC Annual Statistical Bulletin*, Helferstorferstrasse 17, A-1010 Vienna, Austria.

OPEC – Organization of the Petroleum Exporting Countries (2014) *OPEC Annual Statistical Bulletin*, Helferstorferstrasse 17, A-1010 Vienna, Austria.

Organisation for Economic Co-operation and Development (OECD) (1997) *Science, Technology and Industry Outlook*, OECD, Paris, p.231.

Osman, A.O., Louis, R.J. and Balli, F. (2010) 'Which output gap measure matters for the Arab Gulf Cooperation Council Countries (AGCC): the overall GDP output gap or the non-oil sector output gap?' *International Research Journal of Finance and Economics*, No. 35, January 2010, pp.7–28.

Parker, R. and Bradley, L. (2000) 'Organisational culture in the public sector: evidence from six organisations', *The International Journal of Public Sector Management*, Vol. 13, No. 2, pp.125–141.

Paton, R.A. and McCalman, J. (2008) *Change Management: A Guide to Effective Implementation*, 3rd Edition, London: Sage Publications Ltd.

Perez, J.R. and De Pablos, P.O. (2003) 'Knowledge management and organizational competitiveness: a framework for human capital analysis', *Journal of Knowledge Management*, Vol. 7, No. 3, pp.82–91.

Pfeffer, J. and Sutton, R.I. (1999) 'Knowing 'what' to do is not enough: turning knowledge into action (reprinted from the knowing-doing gap: how smart companies turn knowledge into action)', *California Management Review*, Vol. 42, No. 1, pp.83–108.

Plessis, M.D. (2007) 'Knowledge management: what makes complex implementations successful?' *Journal of Knowledge Management*, Vol. 11, No. 2, pp.91–101.

Porter, M. (1990) *The Competitive Advantage of Nations*, New York: Free Press.

Probst, G. and Buchel, B. (1997) *Organizational Learning*, London: Prentice Hall.

Purvis, L., Ramamurthy, V. and Zmud, R. (2001) 'The assimilation of knowledge platforms in organizations: an empirical investigation', *Organization Science*, Vol. 12, pp.117–135.

Quintas, P., Lefrere, P. and Jones, G. (1997) 'Knowledge management: a strategic agenda', *Journal of Long Range Planning*, Vol. 30, No. 3, pp.385–391.

Radwan, I. and Pellegrini, G. (2010) *Knowledge, Productivity, and Innovation in Nigeria: Creating a New Economy*, World Bank Document No. 53645, Washington, DC: World Bank.

Ranjbarfard, M., Aghdasi, M., Albadvi, A. and Hassanzadeh, M. (2013) 'Identifying knowledge management problems using a process-based method (a case study of process 137)', *Business Process Management Journal*, Vol. 19, No. 2, pp.263–291.

Rashman, J.H. (2003) 'Networking and the modernisation of local public services: implications for diversity', in M.J. Davidson and S.L. Fielden (Eds.). *Individual Diversity and Psychology in Organisations*, West Sussex: John Wiley and Sons, p.265.

Ravn, M. and Uhlig, H. (2002) 'On adjusting the Hodrick-Prescott Filter for the frequency of the observations', *The Review of Economics and Statistics,* Vol. 84, No. 2, pp.321–380.

Reich, R. (1991) *The Work of Nations*, New York: A. Knopf.

Ribière, V.M. (2004) 'Integrating total quality management and knowledge management', *Journal of Management Systems*, Vol. 16, No. 1, pp.39–54.

Salisbury, M. (2008) 'A framework for collaborative knowledge creation', *Knowledge Management Research and Practice*, Vol. 6, No. 3, pp.214–224.

Salmi, J. (2009) *The Challenge of Establishing World-Class Universities*, Washington, DC: World Bank.

Sambamurthy, V. and Subramani, M. (2005) 'Special issue on information technologies and knowledge management', *MIS Quarterly*, Vol. 29, No. 1, pp.1–7.

Schroeder, A. and Pauleen, D. (2007) 'KM governance: investigating the case of a knowledge intensive research organization', *Journal of Enterprise Information Management*, Vol. 20, No. 4, pp.414–431.

Schroeder, A., Pauleen, D. and Huff, S. (2012) 'KM governance: the mechanisms for guiding and controlling KM programs', *Journal of Knowledge Management*, Vol. 16, No. 1. pp.3–21.

Schultze, U. and Boland, R. (2000) 'Knowledge management technology and the reproduction of work practices', *Journal of Strategic Information Systems*, Vol. 9, Nos. 2–3, pp.193–212.

SCImago (2007) 'SJR – SCImago journal & country rank', Available at: www.scimagojr.com, Accessed on 3 February 2012.

Senge, P. and Kofman, F. (1993) 'Community and commitment: the heart of learning organisations', *Organisational Dynamics*, Vol. 22, No. 2.

Seyoum, B. (2004) 'The role of factor conditions in high-technology exports: an empirical examination', *The Journal of High Technology Management Research*, Vol. 15, pp.145–162.

Seyoum, B. (2005) 'Determinants of levels of high technology exports: an empirical investigation', *ACR*, Vol. 13, No. 1, pp.64–79.

Shand, D. (1999) 'Return on knowledge', *Knowledge Management Magazine*, April.

Shaxson, L., Bielak, A.T., Ahmed, I., Brien, D., Conant, B., Fisher, C., Gwyn, E., Klerkx, L., Middleton, A., Morton, S. and Pant, L. (2012) Expanding our understanding of K*(KT, KE, KTT, KMb, KB, KM, etc.) A concept paper emerging from the K* conference held in Hamilton, Ontario, Canada, April, UNU-INWEH, Hamilton, ON. 30pp + appendices. The concept paper can be found at http://inweh.unu.edu/kstar.

Singh, M. (2012) 'A framework for teaching knowledge management as a college course', *International Journal of Humanities and Social Science*.

Skyrme, D.J. and Amidon, D.M. (1998) 'New measures of success', *Journal of Business Strategy*, Vol. 19, No. 1, pp.20–24.

Smith, F. (1999) 'Difficulty, consequences and effort in academic task performance', *Psychological Report*, Vol. 85, pp.869–880.

Snowden, D. (2000) 'Organic knowledge management – the ASHEN model: an enabler of action', *Knowledge Management*, Vol. 3, No. 7.

Spies, M., Clayton, A.J. and Noormohammadian, M. (2005) 'Knowledge management in a decentralized global financial services provider: a case study with Allianz Group', *Knowledge Management Research and Practice*, Vol. 3, No. 1, pp.24–36.

Stata, R. (1989) 'Organization learning-the key to management innovation', *Sloan Management Review*, Spring, pp.63–74.

Stewart, T. (2001) *The Wealth of Knowledge: Intellectual Capital and the Twenty-First Century Organization*, Doubleday, USA: Random House Inc.

Storey, J. (1995) *Human Resource Management: A Critical Text*, London: Routledge.

Storey, J. and Barnett, E. (2000) 'Knowledge management initiatives: learning from failure', *Journal of Knowledge Management*, Vol. 4, No. 2, pp.145–156.

Swan, J. (2001) 'Knowledge management in action: integrating knowledge across communities', *Proceedings of the Hawaii International Conference on System Sciences*, Maui, Hawaii.

Szulanski, G. (1996) 'Exploring internal stickiness: impediments to the transfer of best practice within the firm', *Strategic Management Journal*, Vol. 17, No. 2, pp.27–43.

Tat, W. and Hase, S. (2007) 'Knowledge management in the Malaysian aerospace industry', *Journal of Knowledge Management*, Vol. 11, No. 1, pp.143–151.

Taylor, R.M. (1991) 'Towards a knowledge-based model of project management', *International Journal of Project Management*, Vol. 9, No. 3, pp.169–178.

Thomas, A.U., Fried, G.P., Johnson, P. and Stilwell, B.J. (2010) 'Sharing best practices through online communities of practice: a case study', *Human Resources for Health*, Vol. 8, No. 25.

Thornhill, D. (2006) 'Productivity attainment in a diverse public sector', Paper Presented at the Institute of Public Administration Seminar on Promoting Productivity in a Diverse Public Sector.

Tran, A. (2005) *The South East Public Health Knowledge Management Strategy*, South East Public Health Group, Department of Health, UK, Available at: http://www.sepho.org.uk/Download/Public/9443/1/South%20East%20Public%20Health%20KM%20Strategy.pdf, Accessed on 05 February 2013.

Tsang, E.W.K. (1997) 'Organizational learning and the learning organization: a dichotomy between descriptive and prescriptive research', *Human Relations*, Vol. 50, No. 1, pp.73–89.

Turban, E. and Aronson, J.E. (Eds) (2002) *Knowledge Management, Decision Support Systems and Intelligent Systems*, Pearson Education, ISBN 81-7808-367-1.

Turban, E., McLean, E.R. and Wetherbe, J.C. (2002) *Information Technology for Management: Transforming Organizations in the Digital Economy*, UK: John Wiley & Sons.

UAE National Bureau of Statistics (2012) 'UAE in figures 2012', UAE National Bureau of Statistics, April 2013, Abu Dhabi, UAE, Available at: http://www.uaestatistics.gov.ae/.

UNDP (2002) *Arab Human Development Report: Creating Opportunities for Future Generations*, New York: United Nations Publications.

UNDP (2003) *Arab Human Development Report: Building a Knowledge Society*, New York: United Nations' Publications.

UNDP (2009) 'Arab knowledge Report 2009: towards productive intercommunication for knowledge', joint sponsorship report of the Mohammed bin Rashid Al Maktoum Foundation (MBRF) and the United Nations Development Programme/Regional Bureau for Arab States (UNDP/RBAS), Dubai: Al Ghurair Printing & Publishing House L.L.C.

United Nations (2005) *Unlocking the Human Potential for Public Sector Performance*, New York: United Nations Publications.

Van Winkelen, C. and McDermott, R. (2010) 'Learning expert thinking processes: using KM to structure the development of expertise', *Journal of Knowledge Management*, Vol. 14, No. 4, pp.557–572.

Wah, L. (1999) 'Making knowledge stick', *Management Review*, May, pp.24–29.

Wang, R.W. and Strong, D.M. (1996) 'Beyond accuracy: what data quality means to data consumers', *Journal of Management Information Systems*, Vol. 12, No. 4, pp.5–33.

Wasko, M.M. and Faraj, S. (2005) 'Why should I share? Examining social capital and knowledge contribution in electronic networks of practice', *MIS Quarterly*, Vol. 29, No. 1, pp.35–57.

Wiig, K. (1997) 'Knowledge management: an introduction and perspective', *Journal of Knowledge Management*, Vol. 1, pp.6–14.

Wild, U. and Laumer, S. (2011) *Failure of Knowledge Management Systems in the Financial Services Industry*, Research-in-Progress, University of Bamberg, Germany.

Williams, A. (2003) 'KM-project ROI should be visible to directors', *KM Review*, January/February, p.8.

Wilson, K. (2010) 'How competitive are Gulf economies?', *Gulf Research Center (GRC)*, presentation, published 14 June.

World Bank (1999) 'World Development Report 1998/99', *Knowledge for Development*, Washington: World Bank.

World Bank (2005a) 'A water sector assessment report on the countries of the cooperation council of the Arab States of the Gulf', *Water, Environment, Social and Rural Development Department, Middle East and North Africa Region*, Report No: 32539-MNA.

World Bank (2005b) *India and the Knowledge Economy: Leveraging Strengths and Opportunities*, Washington, DC.

World Bank (2006) *Korea as a Knowledge Economy, Evolutionary Process and Lessons Learned*, Washington, DC: World Bank.

World Bank (2008) 'Science, technology, and innovation: capacity building for sustainable growth and poverty reduction', Report Based on the Global Forum on Building Science, Technology and Innovation Capacity for Sustainable Growth and Poverty Reduction, held in Washington, DC on 13–15 February 2007, The international bank for reconstruction and development/The World Bank, Washington, DC, USA.

World Bank (2012) 'Knowledge economy index (KEI) and knowledge indexes (KI)', Available at: http://info.worldbank.org/etools/kam2/kam_page5.asp, Accessed on 24 December 2013.

World Trade Organization (ETO) 'Statistics Database', Available at: http://stat.wto.org/StatisticalProgram/WSDBStatProgramHome.aspx?Language=E.

Yang, B., Zheng, W. and Viere, C. (2009) 'Holistic views of knowledge management models', *Advances in Developing Human Resources*, Vol. 11, No. 3.

Yelden, E.F. and Albers, J.A. (2004) 'The business case for knowledge management', *Journal of Knowledge Management Practice*, August.

Yin, R.K. (2009) *Case Study Research: Design and Methods*, Thousand Oaks, CA: Sage Publications.

Yongsun, P. and Choi, D. (2005) 'The shortcomings of a standardized global knowledge management system: the case study of Accenture', *Academy of Management Executive*, Vol. 19, No. 2, pp.81–84.

Zack, M.H. (1999a) 'Managing codified knowledge', *Sloan Management Review*, Vol. 40, No. 4, pp.45–58.

Zack, M.H. (1999b) 'An architecture for managing explicated knowledge', *Sloan Management Review*, Vol. 40, No. 4, pp.45–58.

Zahlan, A.E. (2012) 'Science and sovereignty; prospects for the Arab World, Chapter 6', Palgrave Macmillan, Center for Arab Unity Studies, July.

Zahlan, B. (2007) 'Higher education, R&D, economic development, regional and global interface, UNESCO FORUM on higher education, research and knowledge', *Presented at the Regional Seminar The Impact of Globalization on Higher Education and Research in the Arab States*, Rabat, 24–25 May.

Zander, U. and Kogut, B. (1995) 'Knowledge and the speed of transfer and imitation of organizational capabilities: an empirical test', *Organization Science*, Vol. 6, No. 1, pp.76–92.

Zyngier, S. and Burstein, F. (2004) 'Knowledge management strategies: leaders and leadership', Presented at Constructing the Infrastructure for the Knowledge Economy; Methods and Tools, Theory and Structure, Proceedings of the 12th International Conference on Information Systems and Development (ISD'03), Melbourne.

Zyngier, S. and Venkitachalam, K. (2011) 'Knowledge management governance: a strategic driver', *Knowledge Management Research and Practice*, Vol. 9, pp.136–144.

WEBSITES

http://stat.wto.org/StatisticalProgram/WSDBStatProgramHome.aspx?Language=E

http://isako.wikispaces.com/file/view/chevron+case+study.pdf

http://www.chevron.com/documents/pdf/corporateresponsibility/Chevron_CR_Report_2004.pdf

http://www.chevron.com/chevron/speeches/article/01111999_managingknowledgethechevronway.
news

http://www.corvelle.com/mini-cases/Minicase_10_2.php

http://www.starbucks.com/

http://www.facebook.com/Starbucks

http://www.sarkuysan.com/en-EN/about-us/119.aspx

http://http://usacac.army.mil/

http://www.usaid.gov/results-and-data/information-resources/knowledge-management-support

http://www.cdc.gov/

http://en.tehran.ir/